I0510428

Mental Models

The Most Effective Techniques to go from Negative Thinking to Critical Thinking. How to Revamp your Inner Self, Improve your Productivity and Problem Solving Skills to Reach any Goal

By Dr. Kevin Carol Miyake

© **Copyright 2019 - All rights reserved.**

The content contained within this book may not be reproduced, duplicated or transmitted without direct written permission from the author or the publisher.

Under no circumstances will any blame or legal responsibility be held against the publisher, or author, for any damages, reparation, or monetary loss due to the information contained within this book. Either directly or indirectly.

Legal Notice:

This book is copyright protected. This book is only for personal use. You cannot amend, distribute, sell, use, quote or paraphrase any part, or the content within this book, without the consent of the author or publisher.

Disclaimer Notice:

Please note the information contained within this document is for educational and entertainment purposes only. All effort has been executed to present accurate, up to date, and reliable, complete information. No warranties of any kind are declared or implied. Readers acknowledge that the author is not engaging in the rendering of legal, financial, medical or professional advice. The content within this book has been derived from various sources. Please consult a licensed professional before attempting any techniques outlined in this book.

By reading this document, the reader agrees that under no circumstances is the author responsible for any losses, direct or indirect, which are incurred as a result of the use of information contained within this document, including, but not limited to, — errors, omissions, or inaccuracies.

Table of Contents

Introduction

Thank you for choosing *Mental Models: The Most Effective Techniques to go from Negative Thinking to Critical Thinking. How to Revamp your Inner Self, Improve your Productivity and Problem Solving Skills to Reach any Goal.* It is our hope that the information in these chapters will provide information you can use to achieve your goals in life.

The following chapters will discuss the subject of mental models. Mental models, at their most basic level, are an explanation of the thought process one has regarding the way things in the real world work. The relationship between the various parts of what is being analyzed along with one's own actions, feelings, consequences, etc., is taken into account to interpret potential consequences, outcomes, and more.

This is mostly a very detailed breakdown of a process that occurs quite organically and seemingly involuntarily. To keep track of mental models, analyze them, and change them is a very basic part of mastering your mental fortitude and eliminating the barriers that stand between you and what you want in life. When you think about what it is that keeps you from achieving the things you want in life, you will generally find that some combination of your mindset and external circumstances are what prevented success.

Knowing this, we take the next step to unravel that mental process. The more factors of which we can take control of a situation, the more likely it is that we'll successfully emerge. That makes a good bit of sense, doesn't it? That's the aim of this book and the information in it.

Mental models are the way in which we interpret the world, the things in it, and the things that go on in life. They influence how we think and our very interpretations of every event in life, while simultaneously influencing the opportunities and connections we see as viable and available.

A mental model, simply put, is a representation of the simple mechanics on something. This is a very broad statement, but mental models are inherently broad, as you can apply a model to literally anything in life. It's impossible for us to keep every minute detail of everything we encounter in the world, so these models act to simplify the more complex aspects of life into more digestible and organizable units.

The nature and quality of our thought processes are proportional to the mental models we've identified and their suitability for the situation currently at hand.
The more models with which you're familiar, the more likely you are to be equipped to accurately understand and to deal with the situation in front of you. When you're evaluating how best to overcome or resolve a situation, the more resources you have to

hand, the more easily you'll be able to reach a positive conclusion.

Most of us have a particular focus or specialization for the models we adopt, which is based on our personal and work experience. For example, someone who works in engineering might think of things in more of systematic way, while someone who deals with children for a large part of their day would think in terms of incentives or rewards. By pinpointing the type of mindset, we have and by systematically broadening our scope and arsenal of mental models, we can see things from a more panoramic perspective. By being able to do so, we eliminate the possibilities of blind spots forming in our thought process.

While nothing is guaranteed in life, there is still something to be said for understanding as much as we can about the human thought process, the patterns it follows, and how you can use that to improve your odds of success.

The term mental model dates back to 1943 when Kenneth Craik, in his book The Nature of Explanation, indicated that children create mental models as a way of understanding the world around them. He further stipulated that humans hold small models of representations of reality that they use to make decisions, reason, and solve problems. Johnson-Laird, in 1983, also suggested that humans create models of their environment and use them in finding solutions to their problems.

Norman, another pioneer in the field of mental models indicated that the internal representations that people create of the systems with which they interact provide them with an explanatory as well as a predictive capacity for understanding the interactions and systems they encounter. The common concept put forth by these pioneers was that models were an individual's interpretation of their experiences and environment and how these interpretations are applied to facilitate reasoning, explanations, decision-making, finding solutions to problems, and in the prediction of outcomes.

Mental models theory also looks at how mental models influence behavior. Gentner and Stevens (1983) indicated that models are useful tools in the understanding of human behavior. In 1984, Kieras and Bovair stipulated that highly experienced users who had complete knowledge and understanding the model of a device were more adept at using the device compared to those who did not have an associated model. Similarly, Fein, Olson, and Olson in 1993 found that individuals who acquired mental models were more efficient in using complex devices.

In 2002, Sloane reported that individuals with more than one model of internet surfing were found to use different methods to search for another internet. This implied that the more models the person had the more options and methods they would have at their disposal in accomplishing various tasks. Mental model completeness was found to predict the trust level of users to an adaptive cruise control system in flight (Beggiato & Kriems 2013)

In 2002, Gentner found that the primary prediction method in mental models involved simulation. Simulating a model was found to predict the outcome of the interaction of the user with the system he was in contact with. It was found that by using stored knowledge, people could simulate future states of the particular system in question. These simulations result in the quick execution of actions that are reliant on preexisting knowledge. Using this preexisting knowledge was found to be related to automatic processing of information which resulted in low effort actions that are predominantly based on procedural knowledge. On the other hand, mental simulations that rely on cognitive knowledge were found to be slow in execution.

The structure of mental models was found to be the basic foundation upon which behavior, beliefs, attitudes, and preferences are built. Wilson & Rutherford in 1989 found that mental simulations and predictions are determined by the structure and content of the mental model. Studies of people in the process of developing mental models have allowed researchers to develop an understanding of the process of model construction. Researchers identified that the construction of a model occurred in multiple stages, these are:

- Identification of the multiple components of the system and all the possible forms each of the components could take.
- Integrating the components into a model based on the relationships between them.

- Testing and running the model.

The rise of the popularity of video games has prompted research into the mental models of video games. Apart from entertainment, video games have been used for educational functions such as training of complex skills, improvement of cognitive aptitude as well as for rehabilitation of physical and mental handicaps. Playing complex games requires the use of procedural and predictive knowledge. Due to the differences in the games, players of multiple games are bound to transfer models from one game to the next. The enormous amount of time spent playing video games has been found to result in the construction of a wide variety of mental models both in the experienced and non-experienced players. However, the models in the experienced players were found to be more developed in terms of the density of networks and the level of abstraction.

There are plenty of books on this subject on the market, thanks again for choosing this one! Every effort was made to ensure it is full of as much useful information as possible, please enjoy!

Chapter 1: About Reality, Belief, and Perception

The reality, belief, and perception are all elements that are connected with one another. Determining their individual definitions, their purposes, and how they interact is a great step to determining what needs to be done in order to achieve the goals you have. Let's break down each of these components and start with a definition.

Reality – This one seems self-explanatory because it is simply what is. It's the current state of affairs, regardless of opinion, bias, preference, or anything else. In very short terms, this is the way things are. Dealing only in the way things are can give us a rather short-sighted approach to things. This is not to say that there is anything wrong with a pragmatic approach to your goals. Being realistic and methodical is a great way to ensure progress is being made, contingencies are being kept, and things are going the way they should.

However, when you're looking at things specifically from the standpoint of the way things are, it can open the door to a measure of pessimism. Have you ever had a conversation with someone about wanting to achieve a goal, but it's like talking to a brick wall? For instance, you tell your friend Calvin that you want to be a writer who is wildly successful. Calvin hits you with a heavy dose of "reality" and starts throwing out statistics of the likelihood that a new writer will have huge success.

Yes, okay, the odds are small. That doesn't mean that those odds are not subject to change, it doesn't mean you can't be that change, and it doesn't mean that you have any less of a right to be excited or passionate about your pursuit. Being realistic certainly has its uses when it comes to being aware of the obstacles you need to overcome. After all, it's impossible to overcome barriers you didn't even know were there, right?

Let's take a look at another aspect of reality and where it can hamper success. When analyzing the statement, "I want to succeed," we'll find a few things to be true. The first is that we're establishing a desire for a situation that is currently not in place. This is the very beginnings of a provision for the future. So where does that leave me in a current sense?

If I want the future to differ from my current situation by containing success, this tells me that my current situation does not contain success. This is where we begin to get into the subject of perception. How do we determine what indicates success and what intrinsically signals success? Let's take a look at what perception is and how that could figure into our plans for future success!

Perception – Perception is the personal interpretation or mental impression of a circumstance or situation. How we react and how we conduct ourselves depends fairly heavily upon what our perception of things turns out to be. If we perceive that everything is fine, we take a more relaxed approach to going about things. If we perceive that things are not going well, we may adopt a more tense or problem-oriented approach.

Perception can really change your entire worldview and the way you respond to everything you've ever experienced. In *Hamlet*, William Shakespeare wrote, "… There is nothing either good or bad, but thinking makes it so." Think about this with me for just a moment. If we take an event that is seen as sad, like your dog running away from home. Dogs are great companions and losing one has been known to be very unfortunate. However, you hold off on being sad for a day or so and you put up posters. Someone calls you and tells you they've found your dog!

You meet up with this person to get your dog back and hit it off with them really well. Now that person and you are friends! What a joy. Sometime later, you find that your new "friend" stole the dog in the first place. Well now, how are you supposed to feel? You're being jerked around by your perception of the intrinsic meaning and emotional baseline for each of these events.

By taking each of these moments as they come, and by refraining from automatically assigning an emotional response to them, you gain more control over your response to things as they happen. You'll be in a position to ask yourself, "How do I want to feel about this?" From here, you can respond accordingly.

When you keep yourself reserved from feeling an automatic emotional response that's dictated by societal perception of events, it can lead you to a line of thinking that might be less than appealing. *Emotions and feeling are the essences of life. If you don't feel anything, what's the point of living? Emotions are equal to meaning. If the things we go through have no meaning, why live?*

This is, funnily enough, partially the point of this. Emotions are not equal to meaning. An event or occurrence can mean the world to you, but *you* dictate your response to that meaning. In addition to this, the circumstances you cannot control in life will no longer own you. You will have the freedom to experience what life has to offer without being subject to the emotions that supposedly "come with" them.

Once you have the power over your response to the events that are happening around you, you'll find a strength to keep going in the face of staunch adversity. To do this is, in essence, to flip the entire narrative of your life. Go from being the person everything happens to, to being one of the first people to bounce back from the worst that life has to offer.

Belief – A belief is a conclusion that one holds as applicable to a number of different circumstances and factors that are based on faith, trust, or confidence in something. This means that we have been given a reason in the past to believe that something would occur a certain way, whether or not we have discernable proof which directly supports the immediate situation at hand.

So how do these three things coalesce or intermingle with one another, relate to each other, differ from one another, and relate to our personal triumph over the circumstances or situations in our immediate environments?

It's true that the things we believe to be true will color the way we interpret the things to happen around us. In addition to this, we tend to behave and respond to stimuli, situations, and circumstances according to those beliefs.

What sorts of things affect the beliefs you have? Let's break them down.

Past Experiences

What you've been through in life will leave you with conclusions that you've taken from your experience. For instance, if you go to the DMV at 9:00 in the morning on a Saturday and the line is wrapped around the whole building, you will probably learn that 9:00 on a Saturday is the absolute worst time to go to the DMV. This is a belief you now hold, regardless of the DMV location, weather, nearby holidays, popularity of that location, and several other factors that might affect wait times. It's important to consciously make those conclusions after your experiences, so you can be sure you're not making any without taking everything into account or doing so erroneously.

Knowledge

Knowledge is the component that allows us to form new conclusions that are based in fact. These allow us to consciously create beliefs that we can use to our advantage in defining and achieving our goals. If we take the belief that was created above, we can use knowledge to amend that belief so it's most useful. Did you know that most business chains and establishment chains have listings with Google? If you do a search for a particular location, you'll see a little graph for each of the days they're in business. Each graph will tell you when they're the busiest.

Your knowledge now tells you that you have that resource and that you can use it to achieve your goal of getting in and out of the DMV with the lowest possible wait time!

Events

Occurrences in our lives that bear a lot of weight, whether they're joyous or quite negative, can cause us to adopt beliefs on a subconscious level. Try to think of something that happened in your life that had a large emotional effect on you. This could be the birth of a family member, the loss of someone you care about, the day you got a job you really wanted, the day of a tragic public incident, or anything that caused you to feel a profound emotional effect. Did you decide to do anything differently as a result of that occurrence? What was it? Has it helped you or has it held you back?

Environment

The environment around us can have a profound effect on a large number of aspects of who we are as people. It had often been said that we are a product of our environment. This does not have to be the case if we are aware of our surroundings. In fact, if we choose only to adopt the changes, beliefs, mannerisms, conditions, etc., bestowed on us by the environment that serves us well, we would find ourselves in a position to control our destinies much more readily.

Outlook and Prediction

Our view of the future is largely painted by all the factors previously mentioned in this chapter. That being said, this mechanism can easily go both ways. The way you see something going (because of the factors above) can easily paint a picture of a future that strongly validates every conclusion, belief, etc.

Because of this, it's very important to maintain an open view of things to come, while continuing to strengthen and validate the conclusion and beliefs that have served us well.

Being aware of the aspects that impact these factors can help you to see them coming from a mile away. When you can see they coming and you know the potential they have for forming your opinions, conclusions, beliefs, etc., your chances of changing those opinions, conclusions, and beliefs into more positive and beneficial ones.

Chapter 2: About your Spiritual, Intellectual, and Physical Bodies

Your Physical Body

We'll start this chapter by investigating the body that is likely to be the most familiar to you. Your physical body is the one you ride around in all day long, going about your business, working toward your goals, it's the one you feed, rest, and wash on a regular basis.

Keeping your physical health in check is an integral part of the success that is often left out of the equation when finding the path to success. Success doesn't come from exclusively working late nights, running on nothing but coffee, and having no free time. In fact, these things can actually hurt your progress toward your goals if employed in any large measure. This isn't to say you can't succeed if you do these things, but you will find it a lot harder to get where you need to be if you do it this way.

Your body depends on a number of factors in order to run properly. The top three things to keep in check for a healthy body are:

- Proper rest each night
- Proper nutrition
- Low stress

Not getting the right nutrients, rest, or hormone balance in your body robs you of more vitality than you even knew you had. If you're getting these three things, you will find yourself much more able to achieve the goals you've set for yourself! Let's take a look at some of the things that can be affected by each of these areas.

Insufficient Rest

1. Lowered immune response

   When your body is tired, the internal processes slow down to match the amount of energy that's been afforded by the sleep you got. Having less energy to run on, your immune system can only operate at a fraction of its full capacity. You might find yourself getting sick more often, and having a harder time recovering from those illnesses.

2. Compromised heart health

   Your heart runs on a rhythm, which is obvious, given that its beat is a large measure of how healthy your heart is. When you're tired, the rhythm can become erratic, which can cause a number of coronary issues.

3. Increased risk of cancer

   Like with your immune response, your body is less able to process or fight through the things that otherwise wouldn't have the opportunity to develop. Getting a good night's sleep consistently will do a lot of good for your body's overall health.

4. Cloudy or unclear thinking

When we're tired, it can be exceedingly difficult to process things as they come at us. When we're well-rested, we might have the ability to multitask, or at least to think in a straight line with little to no issue. When we're tired, thinking in a straight line gets harder and harder. This can have a huge impact on your ability to attain your goals, as you need to be at your best when you're thinking through how to achieve them.

5. Impaired memory retention

Like with our thought processes, retaining information isn't generally a chore, but it can become one if the sleep we've been getting is insufficient. In addition to this, you might find yourself saddled with a feeling like the days are blending together.

6. Diminished sexual appetite

Maintaining your interest in something that requires such an expense of energy becomes increasingly more difficult as you try to sustain yourself on insufficient sleep.

7. Rapid weight gain

When your body isn't well-rested, the digestive hormones we count on to help us process the food we eat are impaired and are being dispensed in decreased amounts. Because of this, you might find that you're more prone to retaining weight from the food you eat, as opposed to processing it as you would normally.

8. Increased risk of adult-onset diabetes

Because of your digestive system being affected by the lack of rest, your body's insulin production can also be affected. Diabetes can manifest itself in some cases of prolonged exhaustion.

9. Accidents seem to follow you

If you're finding yourself getting 5 hours of sleep or less per night, you might find that you're more prone to accidents. Falling, slipping, bumping into things, impaired reaction time, etc., are all parts of being exhausted. Being behind the wheel of a car when you've had too little sleep, especially for long trips, can be exceedingly dangerous because of this.

10. Impaired skin health

Being sleepy can give your skin a dull, oily, blotchy, or unhealthy appearance. You might find that your skin is breaking out more frequently or that you're unable to keep your skin looking healthy in spite of frequent washing and proper skincare.

11. Irritability or mood swings

I know I'm not the only one who can get snippy with people when sleep didn't come easily the night before. Getting insufficient rest throughout the night makes the rest of your day more difficult to manage. Every single aspect of your day is now more difficult as a result of that loss of rest. This makes it much easier for negative emotions to set in with much smaller triggers.

12. Wooziness or poor balance

Like with accident proneness, you might find that your head kind of "swims" from time to time after prolonged sleep loss. This can certainly contribute to that proneness to accidents, as well as its own unique problems. Losing your balance, while in a seated position is an alarming experience.

13. Impaired judgment

Particularly when it comes to the subject of sleep, but not limited to that area, you will find that your judgment becomes skewed. "Who needs sleep," is a question you will only hear being asked by people who aren't getting enough of it. Impulse control and judgment are impaired when sleep isn't utilized in proper measure. This is, of course, not the kind of behavior we want to employ when working toward the goals we have in life.

Improper Nutrition

Your body depends on the protein and other nutrients in your food to keep your body working. These are the things that can come from putting insufficient nutrition or improper nutrition into your body.

These things can come from both overeating and from undereating, depending on the nutritional content of your food, so it's imperative to stay vigilant and make sure that you are eating properly. Keep your sugars and processed foods low, keep your protein up and eat plenty of fruits and vegetables at every meal.

Speak with your doctor for a professional recommendation on the proper nutrition for you, your body, and your lifestyle. Once you have those recommendations from your doctor, make your health a priority and take the time to feed yourself so you don't find yourself grappling with anything in the list below as a result.

Watch out for these:

1. Weak bones and muscles
2. Decreased mobility
3. Increased fall risk
4. Decreased healing response
5. Increased risk of cancer

6. Lowered immune response

7. Pain in the eyes

8. Reduced or impaired vision

9. Cloudy or impaired thinking

10. Impaired kidney function

11. Rapid weight loss or gain

12. Erratic heartbeat

13. Heart disease

14. Tiredness

15. Brittle, dry hair

16. Ridged or spoon-shaped nails

17. Dental issues

18. Irregular bowel behavior

19. Bruises that come easily and stay

20. High blood pressure

21. High cholesterol

22. Increased risk of diabetes

23. Increased risk of stroke

24. Gout

25. Diarrhea

26. Cuts or sores in your mouth that won't heal

27. Irritability or mood swings

28. Fatigue

29. Premature signs of aging

30. Slow thought process

High Levels of Stress

Stress is kind of a buzzword when it comes to personal health. You've definitely heard of it before and you're aware that people can have complications because of it. However, if you aren't managing the way stress is introduced into your daily life, and you're feeling snowed under, that stress can cause many complications that are no joke.

Personally, I used to see stress as an inevitability. It's something that comes from working for a living, and it can't be avoided. This is, in large measure, false. It is true that work can cause us stress and that it will often do so. This is only, however, if we do nothing to manage that stress and recover from it on a regular basis.

Finding things that fulfill us and acknowledging the things that are causing us stress can go a long way toward resolving that stress and to mitigating the effects that stress can have on us. The effects that stress can cause are physical, but since your brain is attached to your mental and intellectual functions, those effects spill over into those territories.

Be aware of the real-world factors that are affecting your internal processes and take the necessary steps to protect yourself from the harmful effects of stress.

Look out for:

1. Body pain, typically in the back
2. Acne, rashes, hives, or other skin maladies
3. Headaches
4. Migraines
5. Stomach aches
6. Feeling like you've lost control
7. Impaired memory retention
8. Low energy
9. Inability to maintain focus
10. Overeating
11. Undereating
12. Irritability
13. Mood swings
14. Trouble getting to sleep
15. Trouble staying asleep
16. No restful sleep
17. Abuse of drugs or alcohol
18. Loss of interest in things you enjoyed
19. Lowered sex drive
20. Lowered immune response
21. Feeling overwhelmed
22. Inability to relax
23. Overactive mind
24. Low self-esteem
25. Loneliness

26. Low self-worth

27. Depression

28. A tendency to isolate yourself

29. Digestive trouble

30. Muscle tension

31. Pain in the chest

32. Raised heart rate

33. Nervousness and ticks

34. Dry mouth

35. Dehydration

36. Jaw clenching

37. Chronic disorganization

38. Impaired judgment

39. Pessimism

40. Loss of appetite

41. Nervous behaviors like nail-biting

42. Depression

43. Anxiety

44. Social disorders

45. Personality disorders

46. Heart disease

47. Stroke

48. High blood pressure

49. Rapid weight gain

50. Rapid weight loss

51. Menstrual disruption

52. Sexual dysfunction

53. Hair thinning or loss

54. Heartburn or acid reflux

55. GERD

56. Gastritis

57. Ulcerative colitis

58. Irritable bowel

59. Compulsive behaviors

60. Circular thinking

As you can see, there is no shortage of symptoms that can be attributed to these three areas. If you're working toward a goal, making sure that these three areas are accommodated is imperative. Look at these lists of things that can be affected by getting too little sleep, unresolved stress, and not eating properly. Can you see yourself achieving and enjoying your success with any of several of these? They sound unpleasant, to say the least.

Your Spiritual Body

Your spirit, the essence of who you are, has health that must be maintained as well. How do we achieve spiritual health?

There is a wealth of options when it comes to keeping your spirit healthy, and it comes down to a matter of what you believe, what works for you, and what you want out of your spiritual health practices. Some people are eager for closeness to a higher power, while others are looking for something that more resembles an inner peace that is dependent only on a sense of self. Both are valid and both are achievable.

Two very key components to the health of your spiritual self can be moved to the forefront when getting started. Starting with these two points and moving further into more in-depth practices can see you through a lot of spiritual growth and understanding. Let's examine these two components:

- Closeness to a higher power or universal source energy
- Altruism and giving of yourself

Whether you achieve the closeness to a higher power through prayer, meditation, readings, or other methods is unimportant. What is important is that doing so can bring you a relaxation and a peace that make the rat race around you seem less hectic. This helps the less important, yet irritating factors of the world around us, roll off of us like water off a duck's back.

Take a look into some spiritual practices and see what fits best with your personal philosophy and your lifestyle. Meditation is a great way to take a few moments for yourself and to unplug from all the erratic energy that surrounds us on a daily basis. The value of this component cannot be oversold; just one book's opinion.

Most philosophies and religions point to giving of yourself and altruism as a virtue of the highest order. Giving of yourself freely and investing in the well-being of others for no reward is a great way to fulfill your spiritual needs. Try taking it upon yourself to pay a compliment to someone you don't know, or buying coffee for the person in line behind you, or leaving a hat and scarf out in the winter for someone in need. See what that does for your spiritual health and see if it's a practice you'd like to continue.

Giving to a charity you believe in, even if you can only afford $5 per month, is a great step toward this as well.

Your Intellectual Body

Your intellectual health is so important. Keeping your mind stimulated and continuing to flex your intellectual muscles is imperative, especially with the wide availability of mind-numbing work today. If you, for instance, work in a security job that doesn't require much beyond sitting in a booth all day, or if you work data entry and there's little to no stimulation, you might feel your mind start to atrophy.

An interesting example to show how much the mind will fight for its own preservation and its own growth can be seen in the people working the jobs listed above. At the end of the day, when they've seen no one, they've just been watching monitors or inputting figures all day long, see what happens when someone crosses their path. The person at the check stand in the grocery store or a friend who happened to call will suddenly find themselves underneath a barrage of conversation.

The mind that had been desperate for someone to talk to and something to stimulate it will unload all at once on the first person who will listen! You will find that, because of the jobs of this type, puzzle games are endlessly popular. Taking a boring ride on the train and don't really need the time to rest? Crossword puzzles will stimulate the mind without needing to talk to someone around you.

Reading books that pose perplexing questions or simply keep you occupied, getting into debates with people on social topics with someone who doesn't agree, learning a new skill or language, playing games (particularly ones that make you think), learning to play or simply playing a musical instrument, and getting into a stimulating conversation are all great ways to flex your intellect and keep it healthy.

Someone who is driven in life will find that they are generally the types of people who are looking for ways to flex their intellect. Everyone's personalities are different, so these things may look different to everyone. Everyone has *something* that keeps them ticking, though. Finding out what yours is will help you to fight any literal numbing of the mind!

When all these bodies are kept in mind and your health is kept in balance throughout all three, you will not only find yourself with more energy than you ever thought possible, you will find yourself coming up with so many ideas and ways in which to be successful.

Work on your overall health with each of these aspects of you and see how you feel when you really try to keep them all balanced!

Chapter 3: About Thinking, Doing, and Being

When it comes to setting and reaching goals in life, there are three aspects that can be seen as stages. Thinking, doing, and being are phases and stages that, while they're not always perfectly sequential, can often be seen to move in this pattern.

When you begin to work toward a goal, you will find yourself *thinking* about it, right? You'll start thinking about how it would feel to achieve that goal or to be at that stage of your life. Then you'll evolve to thinking what it would be like to work toward that. As we go through this thinking process, eventually we will find ourselves looking at how getting started would work.

From getting to that point, we start to evolve into the *doing* aspect of things. We start making provisions, we start making moves in the right direction and doing the things that need to be done in order to bring about the goal toward which we're working.

At the end of it all, you find yourself *being* that person. You embody your goals by being the type of a person it takes to fully achieve and appreciate those goals, those endeavors, and everything that comes along with all of that.

This is a very basic breakdown of the process, so we'll need to delve a little bit more deeply into how these can evolve into one another so you can put it to work in your own life, to your own ends.

Let's take a lofty goal to illustrate the relationships between these points, shall we? Let's say you'd like to start a business of your own. You would like to start a courier dispatch company that people can call on to deliver documents, items, and more to people within the tristate area, no matter the time or day.

The very first step of this process often begins before we ever have a chance to even realize it, thinking about it. Without this step, we would never even conceive of the idea in the very first place, now would we? So now the next thing you think about is how long it would take for something like that to get going at a pace that would allow you to leave your current job. After all, you're not looking to lose money with this idea.

Then, from here, you might go into what your personal role would be with your courier company. Would you run deliveries yourself until you could hire someone else to do them? Since it's an operation that runs around the clock, you would probably need multiple drivers. Could you afford that all at once? Maybe, just to get things off the ground, you could hire one driver to work while you're at your other job, and you could handle any deliveries that came in between those hours.

The next thing you'd be looking at is your rates. You want to be able to pay for your overhead (gas, vehicles, employees, benefits, insurance, etc.), and still, have some cash reserves for when things get rough. Small business is no cakewalk, as we all know.

Okay, so now that you know roughly how much you would need to get the company off the ground, where do you get that startup capital? Do you have any friends who want to invest? Do you want to get into business dealings with your friends? How does a small business owner come across startup capital without involving their friends?

One more thing, what will you call your business? You want a name that will grab the attention of others and stick with them, but maybe you'd like one with more of playful flair to it. You decide to go with ZipShip and you decide your tagline will be, "A to B delivery, all zipped up!" You make note of the fact that you'll need to get a logo made for your business so you can make business cards, car decals, etc., printed for your company.

At this point, you've thought of the gamut. You've asked yourself the questions you feel you need to have answered and now is the time where you shift into the doing stage of things. Nothing really happens if we sit there with great ideas, but don't do anything with them, right?

So what is there to do? This won't be a short list for a goal this lofty, so buckle up! But you've thought everything through and you've managed your expectations, so if anyone can handle this, it's you! The first thing you'll need to do is draft a business plan. You want potential investors to see your thought process, see the model you've chosen for your business, and see a gleaming opportunity in your business. Along with this, you'll want to create and rehearse a presentation that will demonstrate the worth and the potential of the company you're looking to create.

Now is the time when you'll get a logo created for your company, so you can proudly display it on your business plan. Showing you've put the effort into making this company a reality is a great step in showing investors that you are personally invested in its creation.

From there, you will want to get some investors interested. You do the research to find local people who are looking to invest, contact them, get your business plan into their hands along with a presentation from you, and you show them that their investments would be well placed with you and with your new business.

Now that you've got the capital from your investors and you're ready to kick your business off the ground, you hire another driver, you work out your dispatch system, and you put your business's name into the hands of potential ZipShip customers!

Once you have your first few customers and as your company starts to really get going at a steady rate, you will find yourself shifting into the *being* stage of things. You will now be a small business owner who utilizes a very hands-on approach to conducting their business. You are available to your employee(s), you are invested in the day to day minutia that is part and parcel to a business this size. You are aware of who is working when, what packages are coming and going, when you'll be needed to augment or supplement, and you might even find that the other job you had when you began, has slowly phased itself out of your schedule so you can dedicate more time to being a small business owner.

This is not a step-by-step business creation guide. This is, however, an example of how one evolves from thinking to doing, to being in the course of setting and achieving a goal in life. Let's take this to a much smaller scale so we can see what this looks like in all walks of life, shall we?

Your goal is to buy a car. You're looking at something reasonably-priced, but also reasonably nice. Let's say a car that has about 30,000 miles on it, it's only three years old, no previous accidents to report, and it has a large number of reviews saying that it's a good car up to 300,000 miles with low maintenance effort and cost.

So, before you can even come to the conclusion above, let's take a look from square one. You're currently driving a car that is paid off, which is a huge bonus. Not having a car payment makes life leaps and bounds easier. The downside, however, is that the car is fifteen years old, has had three previous owners, several fender benders, and one accident that nearly totaled it a few years back.

Due to the trials this car has been through, it runs a little worse for wear and it doesn't always start up on the first or even the third try. You've put it in the shop several times, dumped just over a grand into it to keep it running, and you still have to ignore the check engine light, that flashes occasionally. While dealing with all the extra steps your car can add to your morning commute, you think, "Gee, it sure would be nice if I didn't have to worry about this every morning."

This is the beginning of the *thinking* phase of setting a goal! You think of all the time you could save in the morning if you didn't have to keep a gallon of water in your car to pour in when the engine overheats, or if you didn't have to allow the twenty extra minutes you add in the morning determining whether or not the car will actually start today, and everything else you find yourself dealing with on a daily basis.

Next, you'll think about what type of car you think you would like to drive most. Are you a coupe kind of person or do you like the idea of being able to carpool some people in your sedan? Maybe you're looking for something with some more practical room and would like to go with a crossover or an SUV. After much thought and consideration for gas mileage, budget, and your needs, you settle on how nice it would be to have a crossover with great mileage.

Now that you've done all that thinking, it's kind of hard not to shift yourself into the *doing* portion of things. "Maybe I'll just check the dealership website to see what cars they have in my area that fit my criteria."

Once you do that, you will likely find something that fits what you're looking for, or something close. Most websites for large scale dealerships will often have a payment calculator that will tell you how much you can expect to pay per month based on your credit and the amount of money you put down. So you go to the site and you do all these things. You find the three-year-old crossover, with 30,000 miles on it, that's at the dealership only 25 minutes from your house, and whose price matches what you can afford.

You'll call the dealership and express your interest in the car, as well as set up a time to come test drive it. You want to be sure that this is the car for you and that this will work best for your personal needs. You'll get your down payment together, all your necessary documents, and a co-signer if that's what you need, and you'll go down to the dealership to get yourself a new car that won't let you down!

Once you have your car, it's all over to *being* that car's owner. Performing routine maintenance, keeping all the papers up to date, avoiding huge potholes in the road, and being a responsible driver!

This is the progression from thinking to being for a goal of this scale!

The thing about being aware of this cycle is that you can know when you're in the thinking stages of planning your goals. You can know what points are crucial to cover in that stage and move forward accordingly. Depending on what your goals are, you can do some research on the most key points to cover in the thinking process before committing to your goal, which will make more economical and effective use of the time you spend *doing*.

Thinking in a straight line is not always the best or even the most efficient way to get into the doing process, but having a structure to follow or guidelines by which you conduct yourself can help you to cover all of your bases, and eliminate backtracking as you go through the efforts to achieve your goals.

The more you know at the beginning of your project, the better. If you're completely educated on something or you're informed of how those things can progress, you'll eliminate surprises or unexpected turns that could otherwise hinder or stunt your progress.

Preparedness plays a large role in ensuring your success in life. The more prepared you are for the curveballs life can throw at you, the closer you become to invincible. Let those frustrating moments bounce off of you and keep trucking toward the things that you want and deserve for your own life!

Chapter 4: How to Escape the Negativity Loop and Have Constant Energy

Finding yourself in the middle of a negative thought pattern and being able to put on the brakes is an invaluable tool that can see you through the darkest moments that life has to offer. A negativity loop is a pattern of negative thinking that recurs over time, inspiring progressively more negative thought patterns as time progresses. It can be a vicious cycle that eternally feeds itself throughout life's struggles, and if it's unchecked, it can put you in a rough spot, to put it lightly.

As you find yourself in the midst of this negativity loop, you will find that it becomes increasingly more difficult for positive thoughts to make their way through the negativity. The good things that are in front of you will begin to seem dull or unhelpful, even if they are the key to pulling you out of the loop. This is where it falls to you to be able to identify the loop, cling to the positive, and bring yourself back up through that spiral.

Take care to evaluate the quality of the thoughts that enter your head. If you find yourself having a hard time, take a breath and sit back for a moment. Ask yourself what your thought process has been regarding this current situation. If your thoughts involve a lot of, "I said this would happen," "I should have known," "Just my luck," "Of course this would happen," and things that sound like this, you're in the middle of a negative thought loop. You are *expecting* that things will go poorly. When you do so, you encourage them to go in that direction.

Let's look at a real-life example of how this could occur with something innocuous and see how our own negativity brings about negative results. We'll start on a small scale. You have found that you've been having increasingly worse service at restaurants and you have little to no patience for poor customer service. In spite of this, you are coaxed into going out to dinner with some friends of yours. When you arrive, the server comes to the table and asks for everyone's drink orders. She's pleasant enough, smiling, and is prompt with telling you what sort of beverages are available. However, you were thinking about how this could go wrong, and you misheard what she said about one of the drinks.

When she tries to correct you, you immediately go into the "I should have known," mindset and tell her to just bring you whatever is easiest for her to manage. Now that you were rude to her, she is less likely to be warm and friendly with you. Due to this, a large part of the hospitality on your visit will be removed. This, in turn, cuts down on the enjoyment your friends get out of the visit as well. Some of your friends might feel awkward after your rudeness as well.

The server brings you your water with lemon on the side and asks if she can get anything else for the table, or if a few more minutes would be needed to review the menu. Having been caught off-guard by the interaction around the drinks, one of your friends now needs a couple of extra minutes to make a choice. The table sends her away, and now you're adding time to the order. The food will "Take forever," now and you'll only be hungrier when it finally arrives.

Minutes later, the server returns to take everyone's orders. When she comes to you, she gets a little bit flustered and drops her pen. Now she's given off an air of incompetence that the negativity loop will latch onto as a reason to continue. You give your order to her in an unnecessarily slow and harsh tone, she writes it down and goes on her way.

Your friends, who know you very well, assume that you must be right about this server being bad at her job, and are overall less warm with her. The meal is not as satisfactory as a result of the negativity you've all been feeling, and the server is left with a low tip percentage as a result of everyone's soured feelings against her when the true culprit was that negativity loop.

We tend to let our thoughts take the wheel, so to speak. We accept our thoughts as the way we feel, and that it cannot be changed in any way. However, there is a process that can be used to pull us out of the middle of a negativity loop. This process is known as *cognitive defusion*. Making use of this process means that you take the time to see the negative thoughts in your head for what they really, truly are: thoughts. They're not the reality and, by and large, aren't even an accurate picture of the current situation because they're colored by that negativity.

Cognitive defusion gives you a moment of reprieve, in which you can take a step back, take a real look at the thoughts going through your mind, evaluate what—if anything—those thoughts are going to benefit you, and choose a better direction for yourself. A large number of negative thoughts and thought processes are not created on a rational or cognizant level. These are inspired by the beliefs, conclusions, and impressions we talked about previously.

This is another stage at which choosing our own conclusions and beliefs become utterly invaluable. In addition to being able to spot negative thought patterns, taking the reprieve that cognitive defusion gives you, also gives you the opportunity to observe and amend the conclusions on which those thoughts are based. When you're taking the time to evaluate the loop, you can take the lead. As a cognizant and rational person who is in charge of their own actions, you can evaluate the truth of the situation, make choices that are relevant to that reality, and move forward with steps you mean to take and thoughts that you mean to have.

Cognitive defusion is a huge deal, if only because it stops you from being subject to whatever thoughts pop into your head. You are not enslaved by your thought process, and you do not have to be victimized by the way you feel about your current situation. Reevaluate everything involved, make a decision to progress on a more positive thought pattern, and find yourself having better results in your pursuits as a result.

Now, cognitive defusion can take some behavioral or commitment therapy to fully achieve. However, there are some ways in which you can work toward it in your everyday life. Let's take a look at what it means to defuse.

Once you have achieved cognitive defusion, you will notice that you are:

- Becoming *aware of* the thoughts, as opposed to perceiving reality *through* those thoughts.
- Noticing your thoughts, as opposed to being entangled in them.
- Able to see thoughts cycle through, coming and going, as opposed to holding onto one so others can't form.

This is the goal we're working toward and, while it won't be 100% perfect from the beginning, it will be something you'll be working toward. Progress in any measure at the beginning is great. Once you can get to this line of thinking, and this position with your thoughts, you will find exponentially more control as time progresses.

When we look at the purpose of cognitive diffusion we find the purposes are thus:

- To be able to notice the true nature of our thoughts; they are simply words and/or images in our minds.
- To be able to respond to our thoughts with positive action if they call for it.
- To take action only on what works, rather than what we feel is true.
- To be aware of the thought process as it's taking place
- To recognize that thoughts cannot and should not dictate our behaviors
- To use cognitive defusion when our thoughts impede you from staying true to your core values.

As previously mentioned, this all starts with taking a moment to pause and evaluate whether or not the thoughts you're having about the current situation. Evaluate whether the thoughts about this situation have a positive or a negative sound to them. Try to trace that back and see where that negativity began as regards the current situation.

If the thoughts stemmed from something outside your control, acknowledge it. Understand that it was negative, that it was outside your control, and take causative steps to move forward from it. What is the first thing you can think of that would be a logical next step from where you currently are, and which will take you in a better direction?

Let's try looking at another life example. You put your car into the shop for repairs. When the mechanic calls you to give you the status of your repairs, he tells you that the junior mechanic on site made a mistake and put the wrong part into your car. While it didn't hurt the car in any way, they will be delayed in getting the car back to you within the originally quoted time. Due to this, you will have to find another ride to work in the morning. This is very inconvenient for you, as your entire routine will change for the day, and you'll need to find someone to take you to the shop before it closes so you can pick up your car.

Now, what happened was *not* your fault, nor was it the result of a negativity loop. However, you're finding yourself smack dab in the middle of a very irritating situation. Now that you're aware that you've done all you could to avoid this, how do you choose to proceed? Do you shout into the phone at the mechanic for the unprofessional behavior exhibited with a vehicle left in their care, ruin his day, then go about your own day feeling terrible? No, you're better than that!

So now that we know you're better than that, we have to put your attention on the next action that *shows* that you're better than that. The next step is to thank the mechanic for keeping you informed of the situation and politely end the phone call. From there, call your nearest or your favorite co-worker and see if someone can swing by and get you. If not, perhaps a hired car isn't out of the question, just for the morning. Perhaps someone can take you in the evening, but not in the morning.

This is a conscious decision to work toward a solution that doesn't involve being angry with anyone, and which doesn't cause more negativity to spread throughout the situation. You can see, from this vantage point that you wanted to scream at the guy on the phone. You can see the thoughts that accompanied that desire and you can evaluate it for what it is. Valid, yet unhelpful.

It is at this point that we must acknowledge, there is nothing wrong with temporarily feeling anger. Anger is a natural emotion that is spurred on by injustices, unfairness, and things that should not occur. It is, however, a very magnetic emotion. It attracts more and more anger whenever it's put into a situation. You will often find that if you're angry, you will either find more reasons to continue to be angry, or others will take that anger as a reason to be angry themselves. It attracts more and more.

Let's look at some of the different negative thought patterns that can occur and how to pull yourself from them. Anger is not the only negative emotion that can stunt progress and productivity!

We'll examine various types of negative thought processes and then we'll go over solutions for them.

Harsh Self-Criticism

It is a fairly common saying that we are our own harshest critics. To further prove this adage, I'm sure we all have situations in which we weren't particularly successful, and which didn't sit well with us. It's easy to beat yourself up for the things you didn't do correctly and, for some reason, it's much more difficult to just as quickly validate ourselves for the things we got right. Due to this, we can find ourselves stuck in a pattern of thinking in such a way that degrades, denigrates, or diminishes our personal worth. We will often find that in situations following a failure or a less desirable result than we had hoped to achieve, that we have the capacity to be somewhat harsh with ourselves or even be downright cruel.

When we find ourselves in this type of negativity loop, it's possible to perceive that line of thinking coming from other people around us, even if they haven't said or done anything to give us that impression. If you're prone to seeing that type of opinion of yourself within other people even when they've never treated you that way, you might find a good deal of difficulty within your personal relationships.

This line of thinking tells us that others perceive us in a negative light, which doesn't give those people a chance to tell us how they really feel. If you're preoccupied thinking that Tom hates you, you might not even hear him when he tells you that he thinks you're a pretty smart person and that he's impressed with you.

In addition to the projection of these thoughts onto the people around us, it's possible for this thought pattern to simply result in a terrible view of ourselves from within. Self-esteem has no chance of growing in this environment and self-worth is almost a laughable concept under such mental conditions.

In harsh self-criticism, we find that it's possible for it to become a vicious, self-feeding cycle. In order to overcome the feeling of inadequacy that we've imposed upon ourselves, we take it upon ourselves to embark on these endeavors to prove ourselves. We're seeking recognition and we figure, on some subconscious level, that if we garner the verbal support and validation of others, we'll be able to see our inherent worth.

However, the support and validation that we get from others are rather short-lived. You can think of it as a drug substance. The effects feel great for a short time, but you'll crash back down in just a while and you'll be hunting for validation all over again. It's a vicious cycle within a vicious cycle. Not to mention that if you get caught in this type of loop, you will exhaust yourself in very short order.

This type of loop makes it nearly impossible to spot our victories on our own and validate ourselves for those victories. Once you're in this type of loop, you'll develop a thought process that sounds something like, "I'm always last," "I can never win," "Success just wasn't meant for me," or "I didn't deserve it anyway." It's more harmful to think this way that we often deign to think.

It's because of this that it's important to put a stop to these thoughts and interject facts. You *are* a good person, who is capable of achieving the unimaginable, and who can create all the good in their life that they want. You do deserve success and you will attain it once you stop getting in your own way.

Anxiety or Thoughts of Worry

If you're too preoccupied thinking of what could go wrong, how badly a recent interaction went, or wondering if you completed a task to a good enough result in spite of it being completed, you will find yourself being emotionally and mentally exhausted before too long. To dwell on such things can more or less act as a sinkhole of energy.

This type of negative thought pattern can come up by looking at hypothetical situations, possible scenarios, or imagined interactions. After all, no one is currently yelling at you or telling you that you've done wrong, yet you're concerned at the very possibility. Dwelling on the "what ifs" can very quickly saddle you with a feeling of dread that can plague you throughout your everyday life.

When you're caught up in this pattern of thinking, you could find yourself eating too much or too little, biting your nails, losing your hair, or losing sleep over things like money, bills, work, personal relationships and more. Your physical health is very realistically affected by these things which may not even truly be problems yet, or even ever. Why should you need to lose your personal health worrying about something that might not ever happen?

Being trapped in the middle of a negative thought process of this nature can make it impossible for you to even see positives when they do come along. Your mind is so dominated in thinking about the aspects of your life that are potentially negative, that you don't have the time, energy, or ability to look for the positives. This is where it becomes imperative to really dig in your heels, identify the thought pattern, and stock it in its tracks.

Problem-Centric Thought Loop

Another type of negativity loop is one that focuses primarily, if not solely, on problems. To illustrate, have you ever found yourself trying to work through something, only for a problem after problem to hit your path, making it impossible? This can be the result of having your attention fixated on problems in your environment, and the problems that have the possibility of arising in your path. If you're dealing with a negativity loop that keeps you centered on the things that *could* go wrong, you're not even giving yourself the opportunity to work toward the things that could go right.

If we consider that someone is looking to change careers, we could see some of the issues inherent in this line of thinking. Say someone is thinking of becoming a graphic designer. They have an eye for design, they enjoy creating things, they have a tenuous grasp of how the programs work, and they have a desire to make a personal business run on that concept. However, when this person thinks about their portfolio and that they don't have one yet, they might lose heart. How do you get work without a portfolio? How do you make a portfolio without doing work? There's a loop inside of a loop.

Next, they'll look into how to start a business for themselves. Do they subscribe to a website where they can sell their services? Do they try to build their own website and go into business for themselves? Do they attempt to get hired full time by a company who will guarantee them a paycheck? Instead of seeing these questions as their *thinking* phase, they see each of these questions as a problem for which they have no solution.

While these questions certainly have validity, there is nothing about them that makes them impassable obstacles. Individually, these are all quite manageable questions to answer. In the midst of a negative loop however, they only serve as fodder for the negativity loop. These are more problems that will attract even further problems. While this is not inherently the case, for someone who is quite focused on those problems, it certainly could shake out that way. This thought process can lead you to see a problem or a reason why something is a bad idea at every possible turn. Success under such a mindset is nearly impossible.

It should be noted that knowing the risks in a specific situation is wise, and that being aware of the problems that could present themselves can give you a head start on solving them. Being aware of your obstacles, knowing how to resolve them, and taking prudent steps toward this is part and parcel to hard-earned success. Dwelling only on what could go wrong, or seeing each hiccup as an insurmountable obstacle will keep you from getting anywhere you want to go in life.

Feeling Guilty or Regretful as a Habit

This loop shares a lot of similarity to the harsh self-criticism loop, but there are some vital differences that we'll cover here. Like harsh self-criticism, it is easy for this process to surround feelings of failure or like we've made a mistake. This loop can often bring a lot with it that can cause us to feel low self-worth or self-esteem, and even low expectations for the things we are capable of accomplishing. In extreme cases, this loop can leave us feeling like we're unworthy or even like we're secretly bad people.

When we're stuck in such a loop, we can become convinced that through our failures or shortcomings, that we're actually malicious. We can feel this way when it couldn't be further from the truth, as we've convinced ourselves that we're a liability to the people around us. When you're in this loop, you can find yourself dwelling on the things that went wrong and why you made the choices that led you to where you are. In addition to this, our view of the past can be skewed to show us what happened in more of a negative light than what truly transpired.

This is a very crucial point: this type of loop or thought process is *entirely* different than evaluating what went wrong in the operations leading up to a failure, in an attempt to do better the next time around. Learning from our mistakes is an integral part of personal growth and must be done so we don't find ourselves grappling with the same losses over and over again. It is imperative that when we look at our past experiences, it is with the intention of honestly evaluating what brought us to the conclusions we reached, what caused us to make the decisions we made, to take responsibility for the mistakes we made, and to make the necessary strides to prevent them from happening again.

If you find yourself using negative language with yourself or berating yourself for the things that didn't go smoothly, you could be doing more harm than good. "Well, if I get results, who cares how I talk to myself? It's not affecting anyone but me." This is false and we would do well to kick this notion away as soon as it rears its ugly head. How you see yourself affects how you interact with others, and how you interact with others has a direct effect on them. If you're stuck in this self-deprecating or degrading loop, you won't even be able to see the effects you're having on others until it's too late and it becomes yet another thing about which you can yell at yourself.

This type of loop, by nature, will not allow you to yell about it and move on with your life. It keeps you mired down in it and everything you deal with will lead you back to the thoughts about how unworthy, undeserving, or reproachful you are. When you get stuck in one of these loops, it can be especially difficult to interject the truth about yourself into the middle of it to put a stop to it. Interject that truth, stop allowing yourself to talk about you that way, and look for healthier ways to bounce back from what's happened in your life.

Identify Your Loop

Like with most problems in life, resolution begins first with identifying what you're up against. This means taking the information above and seeing what type of negativity loop you're experiencing. Once you can identify the way in which your mind is getting off-track for success, you can more easily and effectively push it in the right direction.

Once you've narrowed down what type of loop you've got running through your mind, you can think backward. What is the type of thought that you *should* be having in its place? What is the type of thought that would directly oppose that negativity loop?

Once you've isolated that type of thought, come up with five thoughts about your situation that fit the bill. Affirm for yourself that the loop is wrong, that you are doing the right thing, and that you are capable of the success that you've been working to achieve.

In addition to knowing what loop you're in, it is impossible to note that each of these loops can have a similar effect on you, physically. If you find yourself having to fight with your thought process for a prolonged period of time, or if you find yourself grappling with your own mind, you will exhaust yourself. Getting a decent night's sleep will feel like a Herculean feat, and you will find the very idea laughable after an extended period.

These loops create stress. Stress releases hormones in the brain that break down hormones your body needs to function properly. Adrenaline, Cortisol, and Norepinephrine are three major hormones your body releases during times of stress. These all interact with the other hormones in your body differently and can shut some of them down completely.

Cortisol specifically can deplete your production or usage of melatonin, serotonin, and can cause a host of issues like high blood pressure, acne, weakness in the muscles, dry mouth, irritability, rapid weight gain, bone atrophy, diminished sex drive, lowered immune response, hindered digestive response, and so much more. There really isn't a shortage when it comes to problems that can be caused by increased levels of stress.

You will be utterly shocked how much energy you will have when you kick stress to the curb. Once you amend your thought process to include positive solutions, you'll find more energy in you than you ever knew you had to begin with.

Be a Friend to Yourself

If you can be your own harshest critic, you can also be your greatest friend. You are the closest person to your situation, and you should be able to trust the advice you give yourself. When you find yourself in the middle of an inner monologue, there's an important question I recommend asking yourself in order to determine the intention behind your words. It should put a stop to, or at least shed some light on the more critical jabs you make toward yourself.

Is that something you would say to a friend?

If you wouldn't look your best friend in the face and say the things you're saying to yourself, do not say it. It's not worth saying. There is a difference between being a friend who can lay down some harsh truths that ultimately help someone to see a resolution, and being the person everyone avoids because they can never say anything nice.

If you had a very close friend who was going through the same situation you're dealing with, what would you say to them? If you're not sure what you would say to them, at least ask yourself if you would tell them what you said to yourself. If the answer is no, then you can take those comments and disregard them.

To take this a step further, consider that the nasty, rude things you say to yourself when in these loops, are being said by a little goblin who lives in a trash can. Do you respect his opinion? No, he's mean and he chooses to live in stinky trash. Whenever the goblin starts talking trash to you, envision yourself throwing those words into his bin and walking away to talk to your friend about your situation. If it helps you to write these things down, then do so! Any methods you need to employ to help you remember these things are definitely welcome. This is about you and your thought process, after all.

Acknowledge Feelings

When you're working through something that's got you in a bit of a mental cluster, the first step in the way out is to acknowledge how you feel about the things that are going on around you. It's okay to be affected by the things around you and to have feelings about the situation. As an ironic matter of fact, it's common that we can back ourselves into a corner and feel exactly the way we're trying to avoid feeling. In fact, it can also cause stress and long-term issues.

If you give yourself the opportunity to say, "Yes, this is how I feel about what happened," you can let yourself feel it, process what it means for you to feel that way, let the emotion run its course, and move on with the process of changing the surrounding thought pattern.

Taking this short recess, so to speak, allows you to get back down to business without these feelings coming back up, later on, to bite you with more veracity than they ever would have had otherwise.

Make an Enquiry

There are some questions you can ask yourself at this stage. If you can answer these questions honestly, you will find a more pragmatic view of what's going on in your life, and it can help you to correct the negativity loops that can lead you to turmoil down the road.

Using a journal or a word processor document to answer these questions can give you information that you can access as you continue to grow. As you get used to these processes and the idea of using them in your daily life, you can get an accurate picture of the things that you've done right and how far you've come.

Questions to ask yourself:

- Can this line of thinking benefit me?
- What are some of the ways this line of thinking can help me?
- Can a resolution for my current problem be reached with this line of thinking?
- What changes can I make to my current statements so they're positive?
- What would be the next positive step I can make?

Asking yourself these questions can give you an accurate picture of the nature of your current thought process, whether or not it's a negative loop, and where you should be going as your next course of action. Additionally, you will find that these questions will eventually work themselves into your general view. You won't need to write them down anymore after a certain point, and you'll find that you'll be able to spot a negative loop creeping in on you from a mile away.

Writing it Down

While keeping a journal might not be what you're looking for in terms of ways to achieve success, writing down the things that go through your mind can do a lot for you. As you're putting your thoughts down onto paper, you can assign them to either the goblin or the friend. As you're looking back through your thought processes, you can evaluate the negative loops that have occurred and whether their frequency has diminished, and you can get a general feel for your personal growth, progress, state of mind, and goals.

Getting those thoughts out of your mental space really does free up that space for other thoughts. In a lot of cases, better ones! You would be amazed what kind of mental clarity can come from simply off-loading thoughts you're more or less done using.

In addition to these benefits, seeing your thoughts and your problems down on paper can provide a unique perspective on them, which can make way for unique solutions you may not have otherwise been able to conceive of. Even if you write these things down in a word processor document and save it somewhere, having these things written down can make a marked difference in your day-to-day.

Play to your Strengths

You'll find that a good deal of negativity can come from putting a focus on the areas of our lives where we lack skills or acumen. It can bring about insecurities about your ability to do certain things and it can affect your focus. There is something to be said, however, for being aware of where your strengths and weaknesses are, so you can more aptly play to them.

The main difference you'll find between playing to your strengths and dwelling on your weak spots is focus and intention. You're putting your focus on the areas of which you can be proud and you're making sure that those strengths are the thing that will carry you through your endeavors. When you put forward the effort to play to your strengths, you'll find that you have more time in which you can focus on strengthening your weaker points.

It's key to remember that when you're working on your weaker points, that your focus should never be on disparaging yourself for those weak points. Growth doesn't come from pressure and negativity; it comes from light and determination.

The best way to get started on playing to your strengths is to have a list of what they are. This can be kept mentally, but writing them down might make them easier to track over time. I'm sure you have more than just a couple, so consider writing them down.

When you're making note of what your strengths are, don't simply look for things that are glaringly impressive. You don't need to be a prodigy in an area for it to be a strength of yours. These are simple tasks, skills, or areas in which you do well or excel. Some areas in which you could find strength could be, "I'm literate with several computer programs," "I can manage projects on a tight timeline," or "I have a great understanding of personal finance." These are things that can come in handy in a number of different situations throughout your life and shouldn't be forgotten. Remember that not everyone can do the things that you can do!

If you find yourself having trouble coming up with items to put on this list, consider asking someone very close to you to help you to come up with things. Getting someone to help with this could be as simple as asking the person, "Have I ever done anything that impressed you? What was it?" Simply asking what that person thinks your strengths are can also give you a great perspective you may not have had previously. Plus, it can do wonders for your self-esteem for someone to tell you these things face to face!

Chapter 5: The Procrastination Cycle and Common Biases that Prevent you from Being Who you Want

Procrastination is one of the largest, most formidable enemies of someone who is looking to achieve a goal. In simplified terms, procrastination is the act of putting something off until a little bit later. Ultimately, procrastination creates mad dashes to the finish of a project and creates an unnecessary mountain of stress for the procrastinator at the end of the project.

We know how this shakes out every time we do it, yet we still find ourselves putting things off until the last possible moment. Why is that? Why do we continue to put ourselves into these positions that only serve to make our lives more difficult? Let's investigate something called The Procrastination Cycle.

The Procrastination Cycle is a series of thoughts, behaviors, and feelings that run through the mind of the procrastinator as they try to complete a project or task. According to this principle that was outlined by doctors Jane Burka and Lenora Yuen in the book *Procrastination: Why You Do It, What to Do About it Now*, each person is different in exactly how this cycle carries out, and the timing can differ greatly from person to person.

Some people can find themselves procrastinating over a period of minutes, or hours while some can find their cycle spanning years. Everyone is different, but everyone can spot this cycle and break it. Being aware of what is happening is the very first step to changing any behavior in life. Let's take a look at the cycle as it's been laid out for us.

1. "This time, I will get a head start."
2. "I need to get started soon."
3. "What if I never get started?" This starts sort of a negative loop within the cycle where other thoughts can occur like, "I should have started this by now," "I can't seem to get this going," "Why am I focusing on everything but this," and "I hope no one finds out about this."
4. "Maybe there's still time to get it done if I start right now."
5. "There is something wrong with me."
6. Now that all these thoughts and feelings have come to pass, you're at a crossroads. You must between two paths. The first path, "I can do this," and get it done in crunch time. The second path, "I should just give up. I waited too long and now it's over."
7. The promise: "I'll never procrastinate ever again!"

But because this is a cycle, this repeats itself. Behind that seventh step, there is no action that ensures this is the case. You wind up back in the cycle the next time a project comes around and you find yourself stressed out by this work every single time.

Now, looking at this cycle and evaluating how it works, does this sound like the kind of thing that is conducive to you achieving your goals in good time? Does this sound sustainable for your mental and physical health, given what you know about the effects of stress?

Well, let's look at procrastination as a mechanism. What is it doing? What is it good for? As it turns out, procrastination is a method of stress relief. It's a self-preservation method that kicks in when there is a task at hand that is causing you stress.

This mechanism, however, is a *habit*, which can be broken. Let's break down a habit into its parts and evaluate how we can flip the script on it.

The three parts of a habit are:

- The Trigger – This is the thing that sets the habit in motion. With procrastination, it is almost always stressed.
- The Pattern – This is where the procrastination cycle starts up. You put off the things you should be doing, and you roll down the list above. This is to avoid doing the task that is stressing you out.
- The Reward – A small reprieve from the stress that you're feeling.

Now, the way to interrupt this whole pattern of procrastination is to do a very quick four-step process. We know that avoiding starting on the work will only cause us more stress in the long run, so let's get down to it and get the work out of the way so we can get to the more fun parts of life, and the more lasting rewards that come from the success after completing our goals.

The four steps to follow to interrupt this pattern are:

1. Acknowledge the stress – Be able to notice when you've begun to procrastinate and acknowledge that it must be because of the stress the work is causing for you.
2. Interrupt the pattern – Stop what you're doing. Put the phone down, stop scrolling through funny pictures of social media, and
3. Count it out – Count backward from five. This wakes you up in the sense that it interrupts the stress response and it triggers the prefrontal cortex into action.
4. Take five – For five minutes, work on one thing that you were procrastinating. Getting started and dedicating yourself to a task for five minutes gets you used to the idea of working on it and calms the stress response.

80% of the time, you will find that this will be the push you need to continue working on the task at hand until it's finished.

What are Cognitive Biases?

Now, let's talk about cognitive biases. A cognitive bias is an error in a thinking pattern that comes from conclusions that have been taken from analyzing and processing the information in the world around you. A cognitive bias often comes from the fact that the brain, although extremely powerful, operates solely on the information that it's given and the conclusion that you can make with that information.

These biases are simply the result of your brain's attempt to simplify the processing of information that's taken in on a regular basis. You'll recall that in chapter one, we discussed the differences between reality and perception. This is more of that same concept. When we're given information with which to think, we base future decisions and conclusions off of those, and this is sometimes done in error.

The real insidious nature of cognitive biases is that internally, they look like any other properly-formed conclusion, as they're created in the same process. It seems like you are taking an objective stance on something that occurred and making a logical extraction of the information provided to you in that instance. We are capable of taking in and evaluating all the information that is presented to us in our personal experiences. However, when cognitive biases form, they can disrupt a logical pattern and can lead to poor decision-making or erroneous judgments.

What Causes Cognitive Biases?

Think for a moment about the simple task of making a decision. If you were to stop everything you're doing and consider every possible outcome, every affected factor, and every contributing factor, even the simplest decision could take *days*. This is because the world around us is incredibly complex. There are more than seven billion people on this planet, nearly eight billion at the time of writing. Each person introduces a new number of complexities and variables. We don't have the time or the mental capacity to think with every possibility every time we make a decision, so we employ some shortcuts.

These shortcuts are known as heuristics and, as helpful as they are, they can often play a major contributing role to the creation of cognitive biases. Because of the way we've adapted our thinking and decision-making process, heuristics can be eerily accurate in the conclusions and decisions they lead us to. However, there are the occasional errors that can, at times, feel nearly fatal.

It's crucial to remember that these processes are affected by social pressures, emotions, the limitations we have as people, our motivations for ourselves and those around us, and the limitations our minds have when it comes to processing data. These are all contributing factors to a bias that can bring us more difficulty in the future.

It's important to know that not all of these cognitive biases are inherently bad, as some psychologists believe that these biases serve an adaptive purpose. That purpose is that they allow us to reach our decisions quickly, and to a largely good result. If you find yourself in a situation in which there is a possible danger, it could be a cognitive bias that tells you to flee the situation as quickly as is possible. Now, there may or may not have been any danger, but you didn't stick around to find out. You made your decision quickly and you got yourself into a space that you *know* for a fact contains no danger.

The helpful thing about the psychologists who have studied thought processes, cognitive biases, and heuristics, is that they've been able to isolate some patterns for us. There are actually several classes or types of cognitive biases that can affect our thought processes. Let's take a look at what these are and what they mean.

1. Actor-Observer Bias

   This is the tendency to conclude that factors you've created were in fact inspired or created by outside factors. For example, assuming that your high blood pressure is the result of genetics while you readily assume that the cause for it in others is poor diet and health practices.

2. Anchoring Bias

This bias is characterized by the tendency to rely too firmly the first piece of information you heard on a particular subject. For instance, if you learn that houses in your neighborhood are the best-priced in the county, you may never check prices in other neighborhoods as a result. This is in spite of further development in other areas, new laws and more.

3. Attentional Bias

This is a sort of "tunnel-vision" when it comes to making a decision. Your attention may be focused too heavily on one or two factors while others may more heavily affect the quality of the decision being made. For instance, you want to know what school district your new house will be in, but don't pay attention to things like possible termite damage, or the age of appliances.

4. Availability Heuristic

This heuristic device places more importance on the information that comes to mind most readily, whether it is the most relevant or not. You assign greater importance to that information and have a tendency to overestimate the possibility and likelihood of similar occurrences in the future.

5. Confirmation Bias

   The tendency to favor information that conforms to or "confirms" your current beliefs and to discount information or evidence that doesn't conform.

6. False Consensus Bias

   This bias gives you the impression that others around you are agreeing with you more than they actually are.

7. Functional Fixedness

   This is the conclusion that certain objects are solely useful for one specific purpose. An example of this would be giving up on erasing a pencil line from a page before realizing that a rubber band would do the trick as well.

8. Halo Effect

   The Halo Effect is the way in which your opinion about someone's attractiveness, validity, intellect, and other qualities are affected by your overall opinion of the person.

9. Misinformation Effect

   This is an effect that can color your memories of something which transpired, based on information that came to light after the fact. This effect can call into question the validity of eyewitness testimony of someone who has stayed informed of further developments in a case.

10. Optimism Bias

This bias tells us what we are more likely to achieve success and less likely to suffer hardship or misfortune than our peers. You may recall hearing the phrase, "You never think something like this would ever happen to you," in testimonies following tragic incidents.

11. Self-Serving Bias

This bias tells us to blame outside factors or forces for the misfortune that befalls us. In addition to this, it tells us to give ourselves credit for the successes that we have, or for the moments of good fortune. If you lose $50 on the street, it's because of bad luck. If you find $50, it's because of good karma.

These are all biases that can keep you from seeing the factors that are really at play in your life, or from cultivating meaningful relationships with the people around you. As a result of these biases, you might be tripping over your own subconscious conclusions without even realizing it.

Take a look at these 11 items and see if you can think of any that you've employed in recent memory. The next time something comes up that would call for one of these biases, see if you can catch yourself using it!

When we let procrastination and these biases take the wheel, so to speak, we are forfeiting the control we wish to have over who we are and where we're going. This can make it exceedingly difficult for you to achieve the goals you want to achieve, and it can preclude you from becoming the type of person you aspire to be.

Do you aspire to be the person who procrastinates in every project, who automatically assumes they are correct without evaluating new information, and who doesn't see people for who they are, but for how you feel about them?

Do these traits sound to you like they are those of someone who can set a goal and achieve it without issue? What are the traits of the person you would like to grow into? How could these biases and habits make it harder for you to grow into that person?

Chapter 6: How to Hack the Physics of Productivity and Become an Action-Driven Person

You may be somewhat familiar with Newton's Laws of Motion. Something that was realized sometime after their inception was that these laws could be adapted for use to help with productivity. It can be seen as a huge key to getting more production from yourself and from those around you. Once these are adapted, they became commonly known as Newton's Laws of Productivity or Newton's Laws of Getting Stuff Done.

1. **First Law of Productivity** – *Things in motion, tend to stay in motion.*

   The first law of motion dictates that an object that is at rest, will remain at rest unless acted upon by an outside force. Conversely, an object that is in motion, will remain in motion unless acted upon by an outside force.

   This might sound familiar if you think of it in terms of productivity. If you're sitting down on the weekend, knowing that you have three loads of laundry to do, an afternoon of errands to run, and meal prepping to do, you might just sit right there on the couch until it's too late to do any of it. Sounds a bit like procrastination, doesn't it?

Knowing this, we also know that if you start your day by popping in a load of laundry, you have a much better chance of staying in production until your whole weekend to-do list is complete!

Let's look back to the section on procrastination and remember those four steps about how to bring yourself out of it. Remember step four? Start on your work for one minute. All you have to commit to in the very beginning is one minute. Once you're committed to that minute, you have an 80% chance of getting swept up in the motion and staying in motion until your list is complete.

Knowing what you know about Parkinson's Law, however, you allow yourself only six hours to complete your tasks. This is a really tight timeline, but it's better to run over than to lose your whole day to tasks that could have been done in half that time!

2. **Second Law of Productivity** – *Force equals mass times acceleration.*

So how does this law relate to productivity? First, let's clarify that the force noted in this equation is a vector. Vectors involve magnitude, which translates to how much work you're putting into it, and direction, which translates to the focus of your work.

To put it plainly, if you are looking to get an object accelerating in a specific direction, then the force applied to it and the direction in which you push it will both make a difference.

This, of course, applies to your life and productivity. Getting things done requires adequate force and a clear direction.

If you want to be truly productive and produce positive, desirable results, it's not just about how hard you push and it's not just about the direction you want to go in. It's about both of these things and keeping them both in mind as you conduct your work and keeping them level. The amount of work you put in has to measure up.

3. **Third Law of Productivity** – *Equal and opposite forces.*

When one body exerts a force on a second body, the second body simultaneously exerts a force equal in magnitude and opposite in direction on the first body. For every action, there is an equal and opposite reaction.

When considering productivity, we're looking for things that exert a positive force against the work we are trying to do. We're looking for things like focus, production, motivation, ingenuity, etc. There are opposite forces that can counter these forces. Stress, insufficient sleep, overwhelm, negativity, etc.

So when we adapt this for productivity, we don't necessarily hold it true that these negative forces will always come through in equal measure to the positive, or that they're immovable. What do say is that there are two approaches one can take toward these negative forces, and the approach you choose will drastically color the tone of your experience with them.

The first approach is to buckle down, add more productive force and "power through it." In order to go with this approach, we'll need another cup of coffee, possibly some good music with a great rhythm, grit our teeth, and keep on pushing. This approach can be somewhat of a slippery slope, however. This is the approach that drives people toward substance abuse, and it maximizes on those physical responses to stress that we covered earlier. It's not recommended, but it is the more common of the two approaches amongst the modern workforce.

The second approach is to eliminate the forces that are opposing productive forces. Reduce stress, learn how to say no, change your environment, delegate the number of responsibilities, employ stress-reducing practices, and otherwise lessen or eliminate the negative forces at work against your production.

Once these forces are removed, you'll find that the progress comes very easily toward your goals. It's like suddenly stepping on the gas after freeing your car from a huge mud puddle.

Thrashing your way through the opposing barriers or pretending like they don't exist is a great way to exhaust yourself so thoroughly that you won't even be able to enjoy your success if you achieve it. You're still left to deal with those negatives after the fact as well. Nothing was solved except getting your production to the finish line.

Option number two is the best one for personal health, growth, success, and overall productivity.

Chapter 7: Transformative Habits and SMART Goals

Transformative habits are habits that you can employ in your everyday life that greatly aid growth. Adopting these habits and putting them to work in your life will put you on the right track to learn all there is to learn about something, to use it to its fullest, and to have an endlessly renewable interest in that subject.

Let's take a look at five transformative habits to keep when learning about something. You will want to write these down somewhere and make active strides toward integrating them into your daily routine!

1. **Have a burning passion.**

   Go into the area of your interest with a passion for learning more about it. Let that passion carry you through the following steps. The more of a desire you have to know more about the subject and the more passionate you are about making this a part of your life, the more able you will be to face the bumps in the road.

   People who perform the best are the people who love what they do. As a result of that love for what they do, they spend time and energy on it that everyone cheering them on will never see. Being devoted to your craft means more than simply being there when others can see you.

Take the lead, stay interested in your passion, and develop a passion for being the best at what you do.

2. Dream big.

The dreams we have for the future are what keep us working hard and running toward the horizon. Knowing that bigger and better things wait for us on the other side of the hurdles we face is a huge motivator that will help us to smash through those hurdles. There is nothing wrong with aiming for the stars with the goals that you set. They will only serve to help you.

As you find your dreams set on higher and higher goals, you will find that your acumen and your skill will continue to grow to support those goals. These things are connected and aspiring to be more does have a massive effect on your growth and development.

3. Be disciplined enough to do the mundane daily tasks.

Being dedicated to a craft, job, task, hobby, sport, etc., means more than being present for the parts that others will see. It means being there for more than just the fun parts, the glory, the excitement, and the joy. It means being there for the mundane, boring, tedious, grinding parts of it as well.

Honing a skill or a craft takes hours upon hours of practice, failure, adjustment, practice, failure, adjustment, practice... It goes on and on and you have to be ready to be there for that.

Self-discipline is a huge part of success in general. If you can have the control over yourself to do what needs to be done, when it needs to be done, you have a better chance of reaching unimaginable success.

4. **Be willing to be coached.**

This is really important, so pay close attention: *no one ever learned anything by acting like they already understood it.* Be willing to be taught, be willing to learn, be willing to be corrected, be willing to be corrected, and always be on the lookout for new information on the subject of your interest.

There is no shortage of information on any topic you care to learn, no matter what it is. You can ask someone, you can look online for resources, you can find books, and you can find local chapters or locations that have people who can help. There is always a way to learn something you want to learn.

The most crucial point is to be willing to let someone teach you something. No one will think less of you for the questions you ask when learning your skills. If you let your pride get the better of you while you're learning your craft however, you will lose the respect of others, as well as their support. You will also be cutting yourself off at the knees as regards further improvement or honing of skills.

5. **Desire to be challenged.**

Once you allow the challenging aspects of your craft to leave the area, you will lose interest. The best way to keep a muscle toned is to flex it, right? Think of your brain like the muscle it is. It needs to be worked and challenged and exercised in order to retain what it's learned its elasticity, and its ability to make things work!

Setting challenges and goals for yourself can give you things to work toward and it can keep your interest fresh! Remember that if there is no one with whom you can be in competition, you can always be in competition with your former self. There is always room for you to improve, and you should be eager to take that opportunity!

While we're on the subject of habits, there are some habits that could benefit you as someone who is looking to succeed. These are known as the habits of effective people. They are the habits that, if you keep them, they'll keep you on the right track and primed for success!

Let's take a look at those habits now.

1. **Don't work yourself to death.**

   Striving for a sustainable lifestyle in which you can get all your work done, while still affording adequate time to take care of yourself is the most important thing.

   If you can achieve this, you can ensure that you will be effective in the long term. This is a sustainable, recuperative, and rechargeable approach that allows you to take the time to do the things you personally need to do. Work is not your entire life and you would do well to treat it that way!

2. **Be proactive.**

   Getting out ahead of things is always a great idea. Don't live your life hopping from urgent task to urgent task. Take the time to look ahead, see what will be needed in the near future, and account for it. This will leave you with fewer fires to put out, so to speak.

   Have a clear vision for what your future should be and systematically work toward it to bring it into being!

3. **Have your ending in mind from the start.**

   If you know where you're going, you can more accurately decide what you should be doing right now. Working right now, for the sake of working right now, is a waste of your time and your effort. You need to be sure that what you're doing will ultimately lead you where you want to go.

4. Prioritize

It can be easy to get snowed under with all the things that lay before you, ready to be done. In order to stave off that panic, the most efficient thing to do is prioritize. Find the things that need to come first and get a jump on them. As you systematically work through the things that need to get done right now, you will find yourself rolling into the future and setting up tasks that will need to be done later.

It's is imperative to be able to differentiate between urgent and important. Something could have a timestamp on it that tells you it needs to get done right now. However, it might be something that you can delegate, or it might not be important to you at all to complete. Be sure to factor this into your evaluation before you start working on it.

5. Keep it fair.

When you're looking at the outcome of any arrangement that you're looking to make, don't try to come out on top. Coming out on top is a concept that movie villains use, and it doesn't actually do anyone any actual good. Through litigation and the trouble it takes to manipulate people into these situations, it's not even worth it in the end.

Go into partnerships and arrangements with the idea that they are mutually beneficial for both of you. If you can achieve that, you're doing great. Having an honest mindset when you go into business with someone is the best way to make sure you're both getting what you need from the business and that nothing will go awry.

6. **Hear before being heard.**

Be sure that when you're being presented with a problem, you do your best to hear all there is to be said about it, from as many angles as are available. Once you have all the information, you can throw in your input and go from there to reach a resolution.

If you jump in too quickly in an effort to be heard, you could discourage someone from coming forward, you could muddy the perception of what occurred, it could stir the pot, and you might be missing out on pertinent information that could more easily help you to reach a resolution.

Be willing to hear others before insisting that you be heard.

7. **Synergize.**

This is a very popular word that is used throughout business and strategy. Let's breakdown what it is and what it means. Synergy is the interaction or cooperation of two or more assets to produce a combined result or effect that is greater than the sum of their individual parts or effects.

Collaboration, mutual growth, and coordination will help you to get a greater result than you previously thought possible. If you are able to put your sense of self-gratification aside so that you and your colleagues can share in the success, you will find the success to be even greater in measure for each individual involved.

SMART Goals

Now that we've taken a look at the types of habits that can be the most beneficial to us in our goals, let's take a look at a method for setting goals! The goals that you set should meet five criteria to ensure that your focus is in the most economical and prudent place. Doing so will save you extra effort, and will help you to increase your chances of achieving the goals that you're setting over time.

Let's look at what SMART means!

Specific

Measurable

Attainable

Relevant

Time-based

We'll break this down by letter so you can see precisely what your goals should look like as you're setting them in your day-to-day, and in your long-term planning!

Specific

Having a nebulous goal can make it so much harder to achieve what you want. The more specific you are about the things you want to achieve, the better chance you have of achieving that goal.

You want to state *what* you'll do, and you want to *use action words* when you make those statements. For instance, if your whole goal is, "I want to be rich," there aren't a lot of specifics in there and the only verbs in the statement are "want," and "be." Those aren't particularly *active* words and this statement doesn't really fall into the category of specific.

Now, if you were to say something a little bit more, you could say something like, "I want to develop a new app that will generate $50k in its first year." This is very specific and features words that show action.

Now, once you set this over-arching goal, you can further break down the specifics of that goal. To do this, you can ask yourself some simple questions:

- "What do I want to achieve with this goal?"

- "Where do I want to do this?"

- "What will be my method?"

- "What is my timeline for this goal?"

- "Do I want to work with someone to achieve this? Who?"

- "Are there conditions or limitations with which I should be thinking at this stage?"

- "Why do I want to achieve this goal?"

These questions give you a really great base for understanding your goal, all the intricacies that will come with it, and it gets you into the right frame of mind to begin working on it.

Measurable

Our goals can be hard to quantify when we're in the beginning stages of them. If our ideas are too nebulous, it could be hard to tell if we've even been looking in the right places. Making sure your goal is measurable means taking the time to identify the things that you will see, hear, feel, and sense when you achieve your goal. It means taking the measurable elements of the goal you're setting and working with them.

For this aspect, you will want to gauge quantifiable results. While being happy is a great result for the achievement of a goal, it's hard to quantify. Try looking for something like, "I've gone from needing to walk with a cane, to being able to walk a 5k." These are quantifiable, measurable results that are tangible in nature.

Defining the physical specifications of the goal you're working on achieving is a great way to make it easier to visualize and achieve. You will know when you're on your way!

Attainable

This part of the process can be a little bit hard to swallow. Is the goal that you have in mind attainable? If it isn't, you owe it to yourself to be reasonable and state that it is not currently attainable. This doesn't need to mean that you can't work your way up to it eventually, but if you start to go right for it out of the gate without setting up the preliminary steps, you could be setting yourself up for heartache.

Make sure that, whatever you're shooting for, you're keeping in mind the real-world obstacles that stand between you and that goal. Most things that feel impossible can eventually become possible as we achieve more and as we get accustomed to success, so be sure to reevaluate your previous wishes and goals often!

Relevant

Is this goal something that is relevant to you and what you want for your life? Make sure that you're not setting goals based on the things that others want for your life. Your goals should be your own things that you personally want to accomplish.

Take a look at your motivations behind the goals you have and determine if they're something that is really relevant to you!

Timely

Give yourself a deadline! Remember Parkinson's Law! The time allotted for a task will inevitably be taken up by the things that are needed to complete it.

Put together a flexible timeline for your goal and all the tasks that will be relevant to that goal. Make sure that you make adjustments as you learn about how long things really take, and as you find out more things about your personal capabilities.

Keeping your timeline realistic can do wonders for your morale and it can help you to push harder to achieve the things that you want to achieve in your life. Being too tight with your timelines can set you up for a loss, and that wouldn't be fair either. Being too lenient on your timelines robs you of time that could be allotted for other, more involves tasks on the timeline.

Be sure you're being wise with your time and you will achieve your goals precisely when you mean to.

Setting Your SMART Goals

Be sure that when you're putting your goals together, you're focusing on the positive. If your goal is, "stop smoking," your attention will focus more on the smoking and on the negative.

Base your goal in the positive and you will find that it will bring more positive with it, and your focus will be on a healthier aspect of that goal. For instance, you could be working toward, "six months of nicotine-free living!"

Your focus is on being *free* of nicotine, on living, and on a precise timeline! Just like with the method of pulling yourself out of procrastination, you give yourself a short timeline. At the end of that timeline, you can reevaluate and keep the train rolling!

Chapter 8: The Laws of Laws

There are some laws you should know about to help you in your endeavors. One of them, Parkinson's Law, we covered in a previous chapter. We'll list it here for ease of reference, along with some examples that show you how these laws can manifest.

Knowing what these laws mean and being able to predict the things they tell us to be true can be invaluable in life. If you can see these laws for what they are and use them in your life, you will be aptly prepared for a lot of curveballs.

Let's jump in and see what these laws have to offer us.

Murphy's Law

Anything that can go wrong, will go wrong. I'm sure you've heard of this law before. People bring it up when things don't go their way, but you'll often hear it said as a way to dodge responsibility for something having been neglected or missed. What is does mean, however, is that you can't account for *every* variable that can possibly come your way. This is why our minds make use of heuristics remember?

So, what Murphy's Law does teach us is that we would do well to have a good number of contingency plans or fail-safes in place. If you're trying to plan a large event, there are a lot of vendors, a lot of parts that need to be in place, and there is a lot that needs to be pulled off by specific times prior to and throughout the event.

If anything that can possibly go wrong, will go wrong, then you have a lot of contingencies to plan for. This is not to say you need to double plan everything that you do. This does, however, mean that you should manage expectations for how things go. Expect that certain things may not be in a place exactly as they need to be, and expect that some things won't turn out as perfectly as you planned.

Managing expectations, when paired with accurate planning, will often save you heartbreak and anguish that this law causes.

Parkinson's Law

Work expands so as to fill the time available for its completion. This one was covered in a previous chapter, but for the ease of access, we'll go over it again here. This law is rather handy for people who are looking to manage a timeline or a project with multiple steps.

When we're working toward a goal, we'll find that the time each step takes will expand to fill what's allowed. A good deal of time management and production management is psychological. We manage our time and find a pace that allows for all the work to be done in the time given. However, if we're given three hours to finish a task, we will inevitably take advantage of the time at the front of that timeframe to do other tasks, or to take a leisurely pace through the task.

Let's say you have a newsletter to proofread. It's not an especially long newsletter, but the designer needs it back within three hours. You receive the email and you see that you have three whole hours to read the newsletter.

You download the attachment and open it to set to work on proofreading. Throughout your work, you will find that other emails will come through. You have time to glance at those, you have time to answer some questions for coworkers, and you have time to get a cup of coffee to drink while you read.

You finish up the proofreading and you get it sent back to the designer. You do so in two hours and forty-six minutes thanks to the things that came up while you took your leisurely pace through it.

Now, why wouldn't you just close your office door, read through those four or so pages, get it done, and bounce it right back to the designer in fifteen minutes? Well, you were given three hours. If you do it in fifteen minutes, what's to stop the next newsletter from coming through with a time limit of only fifteen minutes? Nobody wants that.

Sturgeon's Law

90% of everything is crap. As crass as this law may seem to some, there is a fair amount of validity to it. No one category of thing can be complete garbage. At least 10% of each category of thing must have some hint of validity or worth to it.

This principle was coined by Theodore Sturgeon in response to the harsh criticisms the science fiction genre had been receiving at the time. It was widely regarded by a large measure of society that the genre was full of cheesy stories with little to no emotional depth, and no storylines that anyone could reasonably follow.

In response to this, he said that 90% of everything is absolute crap, meaning that there was at least 10% of productions in the science fiction genre that was decent and worth something.

In the time since this principle made its debut, it has seemed to be true in many categories of things that are mass-produced. Romance books, mystery books, comedy movies, board games, card games, racing video games, talk shows, radio shows, and the list continues ad infinitum.

This gives you a good number of things to have to sort through when you're looking through resources that can help you in life, when you're looking for something to watch or play with your family, or even if you're looking for something to guide you through learning something new. You have to be choosy about the things you select in life because *90% of everything is crap*.

If that doesn't help you manage expectations, nothing will.

Occam's Razor

The simplest solution is often the right one. You may have heard of this mental model in the past. This is used a lot for exposition on television shows, and it's used by doctors and investigators when narrowing down possibilities for diagnoses and case information.

When you're using it to help you achieve a goal, however, it can help you to narrow your focus to things that require lower effort. If you put your focus on solutions that require more effort than the solutions themselves solve, then you're investing too much.

That might have been confusing, so let's break it down. Say you're sitting on the couch and you're looking around for the remote so you can turn the TV down. You finally see that it's in the entertainment center, right next to the television. Since it's right there, you get up and you turn the television down manually.

When you return to the couch, however, it seems you forgot the remote and now the show you were watching is over. So now you have to get up and get the remote. You stand in front of the entertainment center with the remote and flip through the channels until you find something you want, then return to your seat.

The simplest solution for this, by far, would have been if you remembered to bring the remote to the couch with you in the first place and not leave it on the entertainment center. Because you didn't go that route, you really didn't save yourself any work.

Think of some situations in which a simple solution was the one that was the most appropriate one. See how this could apply to your current goals and any problems you might have with them.

Hanlon's Razor

Never attribute to malice, that which is adequately explained by stupidity. This model is particularly helpful for those moments when you're starting to feel like the world is out to get you. I promise that it isn't out to get you and that, many times, neglect is the more nefarious motivator behind a lot of the things that go wrong in our day-to-day.

Let's take the case of a frustrated tenant in an apartment complex whose water has been shut off three times in one week. The first time, she was in the shower and was only just able to get the shampoo out of her hair before the slow trickle from the showerhead abated.

Because this has occurred three times in a one-week span, she begins to wonder who in the maintenance office has got it out for her. When she calls to complain about the disruption, she is met with profuse apologies, the sincerity of which she can't seem to discern. The water is turned back on every time.

When her water is turned off for the third time, she calls the front office demanding to know what their problem is, who has a bone to pick with her and that if they'd like to fight, they can fight with her lawyer. Once again, she's met with profuse apologies and finds herself face to face with the maintenance trainee who thought he was turning on the spigot for the hose outside the building each time he turned off her water.

He is brand new to the trade and he was apparently never taught the phrase, "Righty tighty, lefty loosey." Now that he's incurred the wrath of a rabid, waterless tenant who seems to want to have a physical fight with him, he surely won't forget this latest session of his on the job training.

In short, *never attribute to malice, that which can adequately be explained by stupidity.*

The Pareto Principle

For many events, 80% of the effects come from 20% of the causes. The way this breaks down is that 80% of the tasks done in order to complete a project are small or minor tasks. 20% of the effort that is expended throughout a project is expended on larger tasks that yield more of a return.

Let's take a telethon for instance. You have an event during which people are calling others for donations. 80% of the calls that you make will generate wither no return or only very small donations. 20% of the calls that you make will be longer phone calls with people who are really interested in donating to your cause. That 20% of phone calls will contribute 80% of your overall donations garnered.

When you're using this principle to assist you in achieving your goals, it's important to remember that not all of the things you do will result in a massive return, but that doesn't make them unnecessary. Minutia is a part of any project and the smaller tasks are often the provisions that make the larger tasks possible.

Each of these mental models can be instrumental in managing expectations, rising above the stupid circumstances that can cross your path, and knowing how to select the solutions that will most effectively benefit you.

Did any of these principles shed light on some frustrating circumstances that you've run into in the past?

Chapter 9: Break the Barrier of Convention and Declare your Independence

Social convention, manners, decorum, what is considered to be normal or proper... These are all things that society has imposed on us. These are all things that we have been told are important because they are what is most widely accepted, and they are what tells those around us that we are decent and civilized people.

As it turns out, they are—in large measure—bologna. They don't actually mean anything and they don't offer any benefit to us. We tell others that we are decent and civilized by being decent and civilized in the way in which we deal with others, and in the way in which we speak with others.

Certain things that were once social faux pas like having a visible tattoo, your sock dipping too low and showing your shin when you cross your legs or having the right colored belt and shoes, have begun to go the way of the saber-toothed tiger.

People are beginning to see that these things are a silly measure of a character and that they aren't an accurate measurement for the decency of another person. It's important to take advantage of this and really let yourself go for the things that you want in life without worrying about these boundaries.

Declare your independence from societal norms that don't do you any favors. You're putting enough pressure on yourself with the goals you're trying to achieve. You don't need some ancient rules about which fork to use for your salad, keeping you awake at night, right?

It's important to take a look at the things that you "can't" do in your life, and see if they're really things you can't do, or if they're just things that some people say you shouldn't do. If you find that the only reason not to do them is that it might be slightly off-color or it might be considered impolite, go for it and make your goals a reality.

Life truly begins when you start living it on your own terms. Breaking free of rules and conventions that do not serve you will alleviate a pressure you may not have even known was there. These things exert pressure and inspire a level of anxiety that, once it's lifted, you will wonder why you didn't get rid of them sooner.

Take time to say goodbye to each of these conventions and manners, as they have been with you for most of your life. Once you say goodbye, they're gone forever and that's all there is to it. Now you can shine on, you crazy diamond!

Chapter 10: The Power of Imagination and How to Reprogram your Subconscious Mind

Imagination, as I'm sure you're aware, is the ability that we have to visualize something that is not immediately perceived by the five senses. With imagination, we can construct entire scenes, scenarios, objects, ideas, conversations, interactions, and so much more. With imagination, the possibilities are literally endless.

Everyone, in some measure or another, possesses the ability to imagine. Some people have a much less creative imagination, but they can still visualize to some extent. Some people have the capacity to imagine things that would boggle the minds of others! This is why being able to use our imaginations is so important. They can take us further than we would ever be able to go with existing, traditional means.

Imagination is the mechanism that makes an invention, innovation, forward progress, and growth possible. In addition to this, it gives us a sort of test environment for ideas and points of view. We can use our imagination to think of how something could possibly go, and how something could possibly affect us.

Using our imaginations is the most effective way for us to determine what it is that we want for our lives. We get caught up in the visualizing, the daydreaming, the hypotheticals, and the what-ifs. From here, we start to create goals for ourselves that we may not have considered to be possible otherwise.

Imagination can help get us used to the idea that we really were meant for something greater, and it can give us the courage that we need to really fight for it.

As you saw in chapter seven, one of the habits of effective people is the ability to think with the end. You envision what the end goal is and you work backward from there to determine the most direct plan to execute it all. How could you possibly achieve this without the power of imagination? You would need the experiences of many people around you, you would need to read several accounts of people who have done exactly what you have done in the past, and you would need to be concerned with amending your plan at every step in case you were wrong.

With imagination, you're more able to think with the hypotheticals, to envision the inevitable, and to understand what the actions and reactions would be. These things are not to be taken lightly, and they're not to be taken for granted. That which you can imagine for yourself is that which you can achieve. Don't sell yourself short and imagine yourself running the most average bakery in the 4000 Block of Surrey St. in Lancaster, Pennsylvania. Dream as big as you can and shoot for the *best* bakery in *all* of Lancaster, Pennsylvania. You're worth it and you can do it!

If you ever feel like you're imagining too much, or if someone tells you that you're imagining too much, there is a very good argument to be made. Do you think William Shakespeare would have been able to think up his complete works without the power of his imagination? Do you think Elon Musk would have been able to construct his empire? Do you think Apple would have been started, or Facebook would have been created, or that we would have even half our current medical advancements without imagination?

Hold on to your imagination and, I would say, let it run a little bit more each day just to see where it takes you! If you can visualize your goals and the things that you want in your life, you can systematically work toward each one.

Reprogramming your Subconscious Mind

In order to achieve success and happiness, there is a measure of reprogramming that can be done to allow your mind to make more of a place for positive forward-thinking than a negative line of thinking.

It has been proposed that the mind is divided into a conscious and a subconscious component. It is theorized that most of our conclusions that dictate how we act and conduct ourselves are developed on a subconscious level before we even know that they're being formed. We operate off of these conclusions, whether we mean to or not, and they can get us into a rough spot if we're not careful.

There are some steps you can take to change those conclusions, as we discussed previously in this book. Here, we're going to lay out some specific steps that you can employ to gear your subconscious mind toward happiness and success. These are two things that seem to be an endless pursuit for most of mankind, so don't take these things lightly! If you see someone struggling with this, pass this along and share the love.

1. **Visualize what you want**

   One of the most effective tools in repositioning the focus of your subconscious mind is to dominate your conscious thought process with thoughts of what you want in your life. Eventually, your subconscious will follow suit and will push you in the right direction without being prompted. When you're specific in your visualization, your subconscious picks up on those specific aspects and puts them into those visualizations that it creates in itself.

2. **Be specific in the vision of your goals**

   As stated above, the more specific you are, the more specific the conclusions and suggestions coming from your subconscious will be! You will start to see things that look similar between the things you've been telling your subconscious and now the things that your subconscious is telling you. You will be inclined toward achieving the things that you have spent so much time envisioning.

3. Write down your goals

I've mentioned in a few different places in this book, that writing things down can be instrumental in achieving your goals. You can go a long way in visualizing, memorizing, monitoring, or understanding simply by writing things down.

By making it a habit to write your goals down frequently from memory, you will find that these goals will eventually be a mantra that you will be carrying with you over time. That mantra is being heard by your subconscious mind and adopted into its line of thinking.

Your subconscious mind, it should be noted, does not possess the ability to understand or judge. All that ability is kept on the conscious side of your mind. This being said, your subconscious mind does not know what is hypothetical and what is current. It simply acts on the information that you employ most frequently in your thought processes and speech.

4. Employ affirmations

As your subconscious mind acts on the information that you employ most frequently in your thought process and speech, why shouldn't affirmations be a part of that? Affirm anything you want with these. Affirm that you are a good person who is worthy of success, affirm that success is yours for the taking, affirm that your dreams are attainable, affirm that you can achieve anything, and affirm anything you could possibly want your subconscious mind to affirm.

To do so is to fill your mind with conclusions that you are able to achieve all the things you want to achieve in life.

A fairly common thing for people these days is for self-degrading humor to be a reflexive response. To degrade ourselves or to automatically assume that we are incapable seems to be a norm. That is because it has become a subconscious conclusion. Your subconscious mind thinks that's what is true.

It's up to you to tell your subconscious mind that those things are no longer true, and to shift its focus to things that are more positive!

5. Meditation

Meditation is a method that has been found to be incredibly helpful in removing us from the low hum of the bustling world. Taking a minute to connect to source energy, or just turn off our thoughts can have invaluable results that help us to be more of who we are meant to be in life. The tranquility one can achieve through meditation can quiet the undesirable thoughts and prepare the mind for the thoughts that you would prefer to take up that valuable real estate.

6. Talk positively about yourself

When you talk about yourself, do it in the same way that you would talk about a dear friend. You would never disparage a dear friend who is making an honest living and doing their best to be true to themselves, so there is no reason for you to talk about yourself in such a manner, either.

As you continue to talk about yourself in a more positive way, your subconscious mind will pick up on it. Not judging or evaluating the information, because it cannot do so, it simply takes these positive bits of information and transforms them into conclusions on which your mind will operate from day to day.

7. Act as you've already won

Not only does carrying yourself with the confidence that comes from success make you feel really good, but it also tricks your subconscious mind into thinking you're already there. It has no reason to tell you that you cannot achieve something that you've already achieved, can it?

Identify the habits of successful, wealthy people who have achieved goals similar to your own and assume some of those behaviors. As you do so, the remainder of the role will fall into place, and you will feel less stress as this occurs!

Your imagination and your subconscious are massive assets to you. Don't let them go to waste!

Chapter 11: Key Points

Chapter One:

Remember that what is real might not necessarily be what is affecting you and keeping you from achieving the things that you want to achieve in life. You can do everything by the book, you can see no current problems in your immediate environment, and still have difficulty, or even fail miserably in spite of this.

This is because your subconscious mind is creating conclusions that you will operate off of, without even knowing it. You may be tenuously aware of some of these conclusions, but unaware of how to change them, but they will affect you until you can make that change for the better.

If you find yourself wondering why you can't seem to stop a certain behavior or why failure in a specific area seems to be inevitable, you can bet money on there being some conclusion in your subconscious mind that is keeping that in place. It's up to you to make a new conclusion about that subject to turn it around.

Chapter Two:

Mind your health. This is probably one of the most important things in the entire book, to be honest. The health of all three aspects mentioned in this chapter is incredibly important. Achieving success without being healthy in these areas is not only ridiculously hard, but it's also almost not worth it.

Make sure that you're getting enough sleep, you're eating properly, and you're managing the stress that you're feeling in life. If you're doing these three things, your physical body should be relatively healthy aside from any outside health issues from other causes.

If you're meditating, staying true to yourself, and keeping your intellectual muscles flexing on a regular basis, you will find your other two bodies to be in perfect health. To do so is to ensure that you are primed and ready for success. Being unhealthy in these areas opens the door to illness, unhealthy thinking, unhealthy habits, and spiritual degradation.

Chapter Three:

Thinking about what you're doing is the beginning of setting the goals you wish to set. When you employ your imagination and you think of the ways in which things could be different in your life, you'll start thinking about all the ways you could rise to the occasion of making those things change for the better! Thinking about the way things could be always gets us thinking about the things we could be...

Doing. This is the step where we start to make real, tangible steps in the right direction toward a better life and situation for ourselves and/or the people around us in life. You can start by getting the preliminary steps out of the way, but anything you're *doing* is a step in the right direction!

Being is the ultimate goal. You want to *be* the person who has achieved success in the areas you've been planning and working toward. Once you assume that role, you have achieved your goal and you are living your life as someone who has done so.

Chapter Four:

The first step to coming out of a negativity loop is being able to identify that you're in one at all. After this, you need to be able to identify what *type* of negativity loop you're in. Once you've done that, you can dig your heels in, make strides, and pull yourself out of that loop!

Remember that your thoughts aren't necessarily a true picture of what really is going on around you. They are pictures that are heavily influenced by your subconscious and the conclusions and beliefs that you have adopted over the years and through many experiences.

It's important to remember to be kind to yourself, to talk to yourself as you would talk about a friend, ask yourself the hard questions about what you're going through, be honest with yourself, acknowledge how you feel about it all, and write it all down. Doing these things will be instrumental in determining the course of your life!

Chapter Five:

Procrastinating can happen to you just about anywhere you look. It doesn't really matter what the task in front of you is, there is always a way to procrastinate and fail to do it in the time that was originally allotted for it. However, the reason for the procrastination is always the same. The reason is always the same, the pattern is always the same, and the solution is always the same.

On top of this, you are subject to cognitive biases of several different types and heuristics, which can color your perception of the things going on around you. Thanks to these models, you might find yourself operating off of incomplete information, even when the information was right in front of you the entire time! How frustrating.

The positive information here is that these biases can, once identified, be seen for what they are and avoided. Through determination and understanding, we can override the things that have been more or less plaguing our thought process, steer our mind in the right direction, and get on with our lives!

Chapter Six:

Just like the physics of motion itself, there are laws to the physics of productivity. They're analogies for the process of getting productive, staying that way, and getting the most out of the time that you spend being productive.

Understanding the mechanics of what is at work every time you get to work on a goal—or at least try to—can do wonders for getting you ahead of the curve. You will know that all it takes is overcoming the inertia for a minute, getting rolling, and getting out of your own way so that you can stay in motion.

Further, you will know what external forces can act upon your object in motion, and you can do what needs to be done to remove those from your path. Remember that powering through those obstacles will only leave you exhausted or stressed, or both. Removing those obstacles fills you with more than enough energy to complete the tasks at hand!

Once you have the power to get on top of your productivity, you can use the energy that comes from all that productivity to produce even more amazing things that are in line with your personal goals.

Chapter Seven:

Transformative habits, habits of effective people, and SMART Goals are instrumental tools in changing the way in which you approach the things that you want in your life. You will have a clear path toward getting what you want from life, you will have habits that will keep you moving through any obstacles that come up, and you'll have a clear vision of where your efforts will end.

With SMART Goals, you can be sure that your goals have been formulated in a way that specifically makes them more attainable. Following this model will give you the tools to evaluate whether your goals are attainable and *when*.

Chapter Eight:

Understanding the laws that are in play in life is a huge boon when trying to navigate your goals, obstacles, and things that come up unexpectedly. If you know the things that will inevitably come up or which will largely be found to be true, you will have a much clearer path in creating your goals, conducting yourself, and taking yourself where you want to go.

The principles laid out here should be referred to often, written down somewhere you can seem them, understood, shared, and studied. Understanding each of the laws in this chapter gives you a look at the things that are at work *for* and *against* you in your endeavors. This is invaluable information that cannot be undersold.

Parkinson's Law, a personal favorite, comes up a few times in this book, as it really is essential to time and expectation management. You will find that listed in at least three chapters of this book and referred to by name.

The models in this chapter should be employed and understood throughout your goals planning process. If you can manage this, you will often find that things fall into place much more smoothly than they might have done otherwise!

Chapter Nine:

Social convention, manners, what is considered polite, and what is considered civil can often serve no other purpose than to get in our way, repress, and confuse us. We are decent people who can demonstrate our worth and decency without the need for such social conventions or norms.

Instead, we should focus on the things that we can do in our day to day lives that show others we are kind, civil, decent, worthy of respect, and logical with our words, actions, and demeanor. Knowing which fork is used for a salad doesn't really need to be a part of that, nor does shaking the proper hand.

We might sometimes encounter people who insist on the social conventions, but there are always ways to let them know that we have declared our independence from these norms, while still respecting their choice not to do so. This goes very far to exemplify that we can show that we are civil and decent without those very social norms.

Chapter Ten:

Your imagination is an invaluable tool that can take you to heights you might not otherwise have conceived of. The things we imagine to be true and the things we can dream up in just a matter of minutes can make the world a better place.

People who dedicate their lives to using their imaginations to make the world a brighter, more functional, happier, less tumultuous place, are considered to be among the best of us. Your imagination is your greatest asset, and it's the birthplace for every single one of your goals, no matter how small.

Reprogramming your subconscious is possible in just seven steps, which can be done daily. To neglect any one of these seven steps would make the process of reprogramming take so much longer. Working together, each of those steps gives out subconscious all it needs to tell us that we are amazing powerhouses.

Conclusion

Thank you for making it through to the end of *Mental Models: The Most Effective Techniques to go from Negative Thinking to Critical Thinking. How to Revamp your Inner Self, Improve your Productivity and Problem Solving Skills to Reach any Goal.* We hope that you enjoyed the material in its pages and that you were able to see solutions to some of your personal problems within them.

Now that you're clued in to some of the more specific details of escaping negative thinking, reconnecting with yourself, improving your productivity, and solving the problems in your path, you have a good deal of work ahead of you! It's time to *think* about what you want from life and what your goals are. Next, you will want to *do* the things necessary that will help you to *be* all you can be.

Using the information in these pages to achieve your goals is all we want for you, so please go forward, identify your patterns, outline your goals, work toward them, and achieve the success that we know you're capable of achieving.

Thank you again for reading, and we wish you all the best in your endeavors in life!

www.ingramcontent.com/pod-product-compliance
Lightning Source LLC
Chambersburg PA
CBHW070353220526
45467CB00001B/359